Education as Power

Theodore Brameld

A Re-Issue in 2000
of the Original 1965 Book

with a Foreword
by Robert J. Nash

Sponsored
by The Society for Educational Reconstruction

Education as Power
by Theodore Brameld

A Re-Issue in 2000
of the Original 1965 Book

With a Foreword
by Robert J. Nash

Sponsored
by The Society for Educational Reconstruction

Published by
Caddo Gap Press
3145 Geary Boulevard PMB 275
San Francisco, California 94118 U.S.A.

ISBN 1-880192-34-9

Price - $24.95 U.S.

Library of Congress Cataloging-in-Publication Data

Brameld. Theodore Burghard Hurt, 1904-
Education as power / Theodore Brameld ; with a foreword by Robert J. Nash.
p. cm.
Originally published: New York : Holt, Rinehart, and Winston, 1965.
"Sponsored by the Society for Educational Reconstruction."
ISBN 1-880192-34-9 (alk. paper)
1. Education--Aims and objectives. I. Society for Educational Reconstruction. II. Title.

LA133 .B7 2000
370.11--dc21

00-060178

Table of Contents

Acknowledgements

The Society for Educational Reconstruction was founded by students and colleagues in honor of Theodore Brameld in 1969. Nearly thirty years later, Society members and former students, colleagues, and friends of Brameld met at the University of Vermont in 1998 for a seminar, "Reflecting on the Life and Work of Theodore Brameld." Following the seminar, the Society participated in the opening of the Brameld Archive in the Special Collections section of the Bailey Howle Library on that campus.

The seminar was coordinated by a former student of Brameld, David R. Conrad, a professor at the University of Vermont. At this seminar, another former student and professor at Vermont, Robert J. Nash, addressed the audience, reflecting on the influence that Ted Brameld had on his professional and personal life. In the address, Nash made specific reference to the importance of one of Brameld's publications, *Education as Power*.

Following the seminar, the Society's Board met, and having been inspired by Nash's reflection, decided to investigate the possibility of reprinting *Education as Power* as a tribute to Brameld and to the Society's Thirtieth Anniversary, and as a means to insure the continuation of educational reconstruction thought.

We are indebted to Nash for his inspiring reflection, presented in greater detail in the "Foreword" to this volume, of which he read a draft at the "Twenty-First Century Educational Reconstruction Consultation" at Stetson University, Deland, Florida, on January 6, 2000 when the plans to republish *Education as Power* were formally announced. We are also indebted to the Society's Board for its decision leading to this republication, and to Midori Brameld Kiso, wife of Theodore Brameld, for securing the rights to reprint from the original publisher and passing along those rights to the Society so that we could bring our plans to fruition. We also thank Alan H. Jones of Gaddo Cap Press for his continued support of the Society's efforts and, especially, for this republishing of *Education as Power* on our behalf, thus making it available for continued study, inspiration, and influence.

—Darrol Bussler, Chair,
Society for Educational Reconstruction
July 1, 2000

Note from the Publisher:

It is a great pleasure to serve as publisher for this republication of Theodore Brameld's *Education as Power*. I am hopeful that the renewed availability of this seminal work will allow new generations of educators and students to understand and to endorse Brameld's reconstructionist thinking.

Readers should note that we have reproduced Brameld's original 1965 text without any editing or updating. Thus, such usages as "Negro" rather than the more contemporary "Black" or "African American" and the universal "man" and "he" rather than current gender-neutral terms remain as originally published. I believe it will be clear from the educational and political principles that Brameld advocates that while some of his language may be dated, his thoughts and his convictions are not.

—Alan H. Jones, Publisher, Caddo Gap Press

Foreword

By Robert J. Nash
College of Education and Social Services,
The University of Vermont

A Brief Historical Background

Although unfamiliar today to most teacher educators and their students, Theodore Brameld (1904-1987) has actually been one of the twentieth-century's most important educational scholar-activists. In fact, the case can be made that Brameld's activist-intellectual legacy set the stage for the work of such critical educational theorists as Henry Giroux and Peter McLaren, two contemporary critical pedagogues who continue to build in their own ways on Brameld's utopian educational vision. Brameld, holder of a Ph.D. in Philosophy from the University of Chicago, came out of a broad cultural movement called social reconstructionism that reached its zenith from the 1930s to the 1960s, eventuating in the publication of *The Social Frontier: A Journal of Educational Criticism and Reconstruction*, between 1934 and 1943. Along with such internationally renowned thinkers as George Counts (1889-1974), author of the watershed *Dare the Schools Build a New Social Order?* (1932), and Harold Rugg (1886-1960), Brameld emerged as the thinker who built social reconstructionism into a carefully elaborated, systematic philosophy and anthropology of education.

Although Brameld, a prolific author (a selected bibliography is included at the end of this Foreword) and internationally famous speaker and educational activist, rarely wrote in personal terms, the following autobiographical disclosure in one of his last major books (1971) explained why he decided to abandon the study of "pure" philosophy early in his career:

> For one of my temperament at least, I came to find less intellectual and emotional congeniality with my peers in [the discipline of philosophy], excellent though some were, than with a number of other scholars who were closer to the firing line of the human condition. Severe economic dislocation, world wars, virulent nationalism, racial and class exploitation—such issues as these not only preoccupied their concern but on occasion resulted in their doing something about them. From a number of such associates, moreover, I learned for the first time that education could itself prove to be a fascinating area of controversy. And so, when the opportunity arose to affiliate with the education faculty of a large university I accepted enthusiastically.... Despite abundant qualms, I have never really regretted this choice. (pp. vi-vii)

Brameld subsequently went on to become a faculty member in education at three large, urban universities. His scholarship in educational theory, philosophy of education, and anthropology of education was seminal for each field. He pioneered several anthropological studies in education; and, as the sole remaining member of the social-democratic left, he was one of the founders of the Philosophy of Education Society in 1940, becoming its first secretary-treasurer. His first-hand, sustained, intercultural contact with educators in Puerto Rico, Korea, and Japan was instrumental in effecting substantial changes in schools and colleges in those countries. Finally, his construction of an I-M-T-R (Innovative-Moderative-Transmissive-Restorative) instrument during the late 1960s and early 1970s was used to assess the "value orientations" of several thousand social studies teachers, at both the elementary and high school levels, in American schools.

In general, social reconstructionists like Brameld viewed education as a type of cultural politics, as an agency that could be either transmissive or transformative in its overall impact on society. While embracing many of the ideals of John Dewey's progressive education, social reconstructionists took a major step further. Writing in 1947, Brameld argued that progressive education, for all its virtues, tended to neglect educational and social ends, preferring instead to concentrate on pedagogical processes and means. Here is Brameld at his visionary best:

> [Educators and students] must solve our problems, not by conserving, not merely by modifying, nor by retreating; but by future-looking, by building a new order of civilization under genuinely public control, and dedicated to the fulfillment of the human values for which most human beings have been struggling, consciously or unconsciously for many centuries. (p. 52)

Brameld would have the schools and colleges actively involve students, educators, and parents in nothing less than the total democratic transformation of the existing social order. Disillusioned with platitudinous and individualistic notions of democracy, Brameld argued instead that the schools and colleges had a moral responsibility to lead the collective struggle to democratize the economic, political, educational, and cultural spheres of American and international life. Brameld and his social reconstructionist colleagues were untiring advocates of the need for educators to extend the democratic ideal to actual decision-making, not just in the isolated progressive classroom, but to all social institutions, including politics, business, and even the military. Brameld's influence on educational theory and practice continues even today among a small coterie of educational professionals and non-educational supporters.

In 1969, a group of Brameld's graduate students at Boston University created The Society for Educational Reconstruction in order to advance, *inter alia*, two main goals of reconstructionism: democratic control over decisions that affect human lives, and a world community. This cohort of educators and activist-citizens still meets regularly at a series of yearly conferences, publishes a newsletter, and engages in a number of important local, national, and international activities in behalf of reconstructionist ideals. What has bound them together through several decades is a thoroughly reconstructionist view of education inspired by Brameld himself. They are committed to a view of educational change that reaches all minority groups, one that seeks to transform racist, sexist, classist, and homophobic attitudes everywhere. They want the schools and colleges to deal openly with, and to solve, the problems of corporate hegemony, poverty, inequality, suppression of human rights, war, and greed. They urge that political and economic power be extended to the ordinary person on Main Street rather than controlled by the moguls on Wall Street. For the Society of Educational Reconstruction, political knowledge and political action cannot be separated. Thus, educators are always social activists, whether they know it or not, because they are consciously or unconsciously acting either to conserve or to transform the status quo. *Education as Power* serves as an excellent encapsulation and elaboration of all of these themes.

My Initial, Personal Encounter With Ted Brameld

I first met Ted Brameld in the early fall of 1965. I remember waiting anxiously outside his office door as I was about to begin my doctoral studies in philosophy of education at Boston University. My intent was to ask him to be my advisor for the duration of my program. This was a huge risk for me to take because if he had said no, I am sure that feeling rejected and unworthy, I would have walked away from the university for good. Here I was, a working-class, twenty-something, first-generation college graduate, who had never been outside the New England area. I was approaching an internationally famous scholar who, in addition to his many educational accomplishments in the United States, was also working to change the face of schooling in Japan, Korea, and Puerto Rico.

When I finally got to meet him that fall afternoon, I recall stammering something silly like "Hello, Professor Brameld, I want to study with you, because you come highly recommended." The fact was that I had read much of Ted's work as a Master's student in English at another university, and I was overwhelmed with his vision, integrity, and intellectual brilliance. Having had no background at all in philosophy, at first I found his ideas dense and difficult to navigate. After a while, however, the complex concepts began to make sense. During that first meeting with Ted, I tried awkwardly to tell him what I liked about his thinking, but my effort was mostly in vain. I was simply too nervous to impress him. Graciously but discerningly, Ted put me at ease: "I'd be pleased to have you as my advisee. You need to know, however, that you don't have to be a True Believer to work with me. Just read carefully, listen patiently, and make up your own mind about the validity of my ideas. Believe it or not, I look forward to learning as much from you as you do from me."

I left Ted's office feeling great relief. Not only was I about to embark on an intensive, three-year, intellectual journey with the leading philosopher of education in the country, but I knew I would like this man as a person. And, happily, I sensed he might even like me as well. While I could hardly be aware of it at the time, and despite many philosophico-political fits and starts over the next three decades, Ted Brameld was about to change the course of my entire life. (For starters, I became the first president of The Society for Educational Reconstruction in Boston in 1969.) Today, some 35 years later, I marvel at how profoundly Ted has left his mark on my scholarship, teaching, and overall philosophy of life. Thus, it is a great honor to write a Foreword to this re-issue of *Education as Power*, first published in 1965, because, in my opinion, the book is a wonderfully accessible summary of much of what Ted Brameld stood for as an educator over the course of his lengthy career. Despite its brevity, and its early 1960s, cold-war perspective on geo-politics and education, I still find the volume to be incredibly relevant to many of today's, 21st century, educational concerns.

Because the essays were originally delivered as a series of on-location, spontaneously translated lectures to educators and lay leaders in Korea, the writing style is conversational, clear, and non-technical. Also, because Ted Brameld was a genuine visionary, many of the ideas in this short text—radical at the time—have proven to be surprisingly prescient. And, finally, because his work was always so controversial among certain conservative sectors in educational philosophy, Ted meant for this book to be a series of succinct, emended responses to many detractors' critiques of his major ideas. In the following sections, I will briefly summarize the three main themes in *Education as Power*—Educational Crisis, Educational Reconstructionism, and Values Education. As best I can in a short Foreword, I will mention what I think is their continuing relevance for educational theory and practice in the new millennium. Finally, I will close with a short, personal reflection regarding Ted Brameld's enormous impact on my own life.

Educational Crisis

Brameld continued to insist in this book, as in all of his others, that American society, and the educational system that characterized it, was in crisis. For Brameld, a thinker whose philosophy of education was profoundly informed by an anthropological perspective, "crisis connotes a major dislocation—a dislocation of the fundamental institutions, habits, practices, attitudes of any given culture or any section of a culture." Even though in the early 1960s the veneer of American life looked relatively calm, Brameld pointed out that in actuality seven areas (science, economics, human relations, arts, religion, politics, and education) of American culture were suffering from severe dislocations. Most of his observations ring true even today.

For example, while *science* has given us much by way of medical and technological breakthroughs to make life more livable and convenient, it has also been responsible for the invention of terrible military weapons, including nuclear armaments (what political leaders now call "weapons of mass destruction"), which to this day threaten human life and the natural environment everywhere on earth. Brameld warned in *Education as Power* that scientists must never again hide behind the myth of scientific objectivity as an excuse to ignore their moral responsibility for producing, and testing, atomic, hydrogen, and cobalt bombs, and the terrible genetic defects and environmental devastation that have been their aftermath. Given the continued growth of the world-wide weapons industry, arms trading, and nuclear stockpiling at the present time, Brameld was right to be gravely concerned about science's ethical obligations.

In the area of *economics* in the 1960s, Brameld pointed out that in the interests of efficiency, the growth of automation in factories, particularly in the inner cities, had resulted in massive unemployment for minorities. Today, of course, in the name of corporate efficiency and profit maximization, automation has brought about a rash of "downsizing" and "right-sizing," affecting not only the white and minority working classes but the elite career class as well. Brameld would especially deplore the growing chasm between America's haves and have-nots at the present time, despite the popularity of stock-inflated 401K retirement plans among a privileged group of middle-class professionals. He would remind us that a soaring DOW, NASDAQ, and S&P investment market, along with the instant creation of internet and bio-technology millionaires, has done little to rectify the plight of the homeless, or the crisis in health care whose disastrous effects are disproportionately shared by the young, the poor, and the elderly of all races and ethnicities, or the steady degeneration of education in inner cities and rural areas throughout the United States.

In the area of *human relations*, Brameld was acutely troubled by the continuing conflict between the white and black races, which he felt were "more acutely dislocated now [in the 1960s] than at any time since the Civil War." Today, in spite of all the promising activity in the schools and colleges around multiculturalism, diversity, and cultural pluralism, the divide between the different races, ethnicities, genders, sexual orientations, religions, and social classes continues to widen in America, particularly in major urban and suburban areas. Many of the nation's colleges and universities are systematically dismantling Affirmative Action programs. Bigotry, hatred, and ignorance pervade our schools and colleges, as incidents of hate speech, outright acts of violence, and insidious forms of discrimination proliferate in every one of this nation's cultural institutions. I suspect that, even though Brameld was an unflappable realist, he would still be shocked at the extent of America's deep-seated fear and hatred of "otherness" in the early 21st century.

Regarding the *arts* in the early 1960s, Brameld worried over the decreasing federal expenditures on all the arts in America, as well as the continuing recurrence of such existential themes in the arts as absurdity, anxiety, and meaninglessness—"barometers of an anguished and alienated spirit" in America. Today, Brameld would probably agree that postmodern art is still a dependable barometer of Western life. For the most part, postmodern art—particularly in its mass culture manifestations—reflects the relativism and nihilism of American culture, and, increasingly, it is being used to deconstruct, rather than reconstruct, all the allegedly great artistic "texts" of the Western heritage. And in some educational sectors, in the hands of both the left and the right, art has become little more than a crude political tool meant to advance a particular ideology.

Brameld was adamant that the study of the arts must become the study of life. Art is a wonderful way to unify all elements of a curriculum, because art touches every aspect of our lives, including our education, our recreation, our politics, our philosophies, our literature, and our religions. At times art inspires and uplifts the human spirit; at other times it soothes and it outrages. Often it innovates; so too does it imitate. Unlike science, according to Brameld, art is "unrational," existential, emotional, occasionally even "Zen-like." Brameld constantly reminded teachers that students needed to understand the complex interconnections between art and all other areas of human activity. This, for him, entailed the asking of such politically-loaded questions as whether radio and television, and museums and theaters, should become publicly owned and controlled.

In the area of *religion*, Brameld saw much hypocrisy in those 1960s church joiners who appeared more intent on using a conspicuous religiosity to achieve upward mobility instead of genuine spiritual nourishment. Today, while recent Gallup opinion polls suggest that Americans appear to be turning back in droves to organized religion for a sense of direction and meaning in their lives, the reality is somewhat more ambiguous, and, in fact, closer to Brameld's insights on the issue. The same polls show that people prefer a kind of generic, private spirituality over membership in a mainline religious tradition. The majority of American church-goers do not believe in moral absolutes; they maintain that they can be religious without attending a church or a synagogue; and they have little or no confidence in the clergy (Nash, 1999). While an amorphous, New Age personal spirituality flourishes at this time, the more liberal Protestant and Catholic churches in this country continue to decline in membership. Ironically, in response to what they perceive to be the moral nihilism of modernism and postmodernism, the far more conservative Pentecostal, Fundamentalist, and Evangelical communities appear to be thriving, both in America and throughout the world.

And *politically*, in the early 1960s, Brameld worried that the clash between the nationalists and the internationalists at the highest levels of government in establishing foreign policy was not just prolonging the cold war; it was exacerbating beyond repair tensions between the Soviet Union and the West, with the prospect of nuclear devastation always a looming possibility. Today, with the cold war over, the Berlin Wall long-since demolished, and the old Soviet Union fractionated beyond repair, new, more frightening dangers appear on the international horizon. An increasing number of nations have become nuclearized. There has been a resurgence of neo-communist and neo-fascist political movements throughout the globe. The recent military interventions of the United Nations and the United States to protect sovereign nations from their internal and external enemies have often made things worse in these countries. Religious fundamentalism as a reaction to the excesses of Western modernism has become a worldwide phenomenon, particularly in many Christian, Islamic, and Hindu states. And China is fast becoming a world economic and military power with strong antagonisms to what it regards as the imperialism of Western democracies.

Educational Reconstructionism

For Brameld, only a "reconstructed philosophy of education" was able to respond effectively to the crises of culture cited above. Brameld used a portion of *Education as Power* to vindicate his career-long use of four "cultural interpretations of education": *perennialism*, *essentialism*, *progressivism*, and *reconstructionism*. In reaction to his critics who believed that these labels were nothing more than artificial catch-alls that failed to capture the genuine complexities of education and politics, Brameld insisted that such categories were still highly serviceable to educational theorists. After painstaking rethinking in a number of theoretical works during the later stages of his career, Brameld remained convinced in *Education as Power* that educational responses to the crises described in the previous section made sense only when they were understood as "cultural interpretations." The major change in Brameld's approach in using these categories in *Education as Power* was to join them in pairs (perennialist-essentialist and progressivist-reconstructionist) in order to emphasize their commonalities as well as their differences. In more contemporary, postmodern language, what Brameld is saying is that the way educators approach cultural crises is inescapably influenced by the philosophical "paradigms" they construct. Paradigms represent the hidden assumptions, perspectives, values, and biases that determine how educators make sense of the world, as well as how they distinguish what is important to teach, and what course of action they should take to achieve their goals.

Thus, the perennialist-essentialist paradigm is typically traditional: subject-centered, skill- and technology-based, fact-dominant, culture conserving, and grounded in absolute truths; while the progressivist-reconstructionist paradigm is experimental and political: student-centered, community- and problem-based, scientific, humanistic, radically democratic, and values-driven. Once again, in more contemporary terms, perennialism-essentialism is a view of objective reality that is mainly *mind-independent* or objectivist, one where the educator's responsibility is to teach students to discover the eternal, unchanging realities in a world that exists as largely independent of the mind. And progressivism-reconstructionism is a perspective on the world that is *mind-dependent* or constructivist, where the educator's responsibility is to teach students to understand the world as a social construction, shaped, in part, by the perspectives, means, and purposes that students bring to it. Thus, at least in theory, students possess the power to help create a better world than the one they currently inhabit.

In my own opinion, I believe that Brameld's paradigms continue to hold up very well at the beginning of the 21st century. Without concise, simplified paradigms in education, as in all the sciences, social sciences, and humanities, it is exceedingly difficult to make crucial distinctions; without them, we have no functional maps for "reading" the reality of schooling in America. Thomas Kuhn (1970) has shown how science has progressed through the centuries by displacing one paradigm with another. Brameld argues in this book that most of what educators say about their beliefs and practices is, in the end, conditioned directly or indirectly by either one of these two cultural paradigms. He also believes that the progressivist-reconstructionist paradigm has supplanted the perennialist-essentialist one as a more satisfactory educational cartography for a troubled modern world. Moreover, educators have an obligation to indicate to students and parents where they stand on these two paradigms, because no educator can ever be truly impartial. In fact, Brameld contends that educators have a moral and professional responsibility to make their "partialities [paradigms] defensible" by arguing clearly, respectfully, and persuasively for their particular "cartography" in regard to the crises outlined earlier.

Brameld's exciting message in *Education as Power*, as in so many of his other writings, is that education as the great "transmitting and modifying agency of culture" is inescapably involved with all the above-mentioned crisis areas, whether or not it wants to be. In the early 1960s, Brameld felt that, by and large, education's response to cultural crisis was grossly inadequate. For him, education opted to ignore cultural crises by aligning itself with established power structures—e.g., by preparing "gifted" students to maintain American technological and military superiority. Or else education sought to rise above these cultural dislocations by becoming highly reactionary—intellectualistic and bookish. In contrast, for Brameld, if education was to be truly "powerful," it had to be an education directed mainly toward achieving worthwhile socio-political ends. Brameld's major goal for a "reconstructed philosophy of education" was the "building of a world order of nations under the direction of the majority of peoples." For Brameld, educational means, no matter how "practical" or "progressive," were always "blind"—absent the powerful, world-building ends required to drive them.

While the present-day reader might reasonably argue that the post-cold war multiplication of ethnic, religious, and nationalistic "civilizations" has invalidated Brameld's euphoric dream of One-World government, if he were alive today, I do not think he would back away. He would continue to insist that only an international world body of some kind—where nations make the continuing commitment to live side-by-side in cooperative interchange in order to learn from each other's successes and mistakes in history, art, culture, education, politics, and economics—is the best safeguard against ethnic cleansing, the breakdown of law and order, costly local and national wars of attrition, and the ultimate catastrophe of nuclear destruction. And, as always, Brameld would place the schools and colleges at the center of his efforts to construct a more humane world, because, in his eyes, education and culture were virtually inseparable.

Cultures are dependent on their educational institutions both to transmit what is good and to transform what is bad, if they are to survive and prosper. Thus, if there is institutional disequilibrium, moral confusion, and uncertainty in the culture at large, then, as always, it is education's obligation to be both a transmissive *and* a transformative cultural agency. As in the 1960s, so too today, Brameld's mandate to "enlist and unite the majority of peoples of all races, religions, and nationalities into a great democratic world body with power and authority to enforce its policies" would become an educational ideal animating all aspects of American schooling.

The ultimate test for Brameld of whether American education is doing its job well is the extent to which it is able to help students of all ages to diagnose and to rectify all the cultural "disequilibriums" mentioned in the previous section. Underlying Brameld's democratic ideal for American education is his unwavering faith that, with effective schooling, ordinary human beings possess the common sense and good judgment to govern themselves far better than elite leaders or groups of leaders. Today, in an era of special-interest groups in politics, business cabals, government and judicial usurpation of individual decision-making, and superauthorities of all types in the media and in the professions, Brameld's trust in the wisdom of the common person is genuinely counter-cultural.

Thus, I am certain that Brameld's "reconstructed philosophy of education" for today's schools and colleges would be *political* through and through. He would not backtrack on his belief that students must learn how to implement what he called a "bi-polar" philosophy of democracy: knowing how to engage intelligently and persuasively in policy making, but also knowing how to dissent respectfully and constructively from the policies established by the majority, whenever this is morally and politically required. America's schools and colleges would stand for something far more important than mere preparation for individual careerism. Education everywhere would concentrate on current events, particularly those important, world-wide, socio-political events that affect nations and whole civilizations.

This kind of education would be visionary, pragmatic, and critical-minded. It would urge teachers and students to identify the moral and religious values that human beings throughout the world share in common despite their cultural differences. I also think that, given Brameld's willingness to constantly revise his reconstructionist paradigm, he would advocate a democratic decision-making process for all peoples that was less universalistic and prescriptive in design than earlier. This up-dated paradigm, more complex than the one he proffered in the dualistic (West vs. Russia) geo-political arrangements of the 1960s, would be considerably more sensitive to the religio-political diversities that characterize a third-millennium, multi-civilizational (Western, Latin American, African, Islamic, Sinic, Hindu, Orthodox, Buddhist, and Japanese) world. At the present time, many of these "civilizations" deeply resent the "imperialism of democracy" that they believe drives the world-wide political agenda of the United States and other Western nations (see Huntington, 1996).

As sweeping and as visionary as it was, Brameld never meant for his educational reconstructionism to be a stand-pat paradigm, however. In response to those critics who accused him of creating a "completed" theory, he responded that reconstructionist educators must continually take responsibility for transforming their paradigm, whenever it was no longer capable of explaining new cultural phenomena. In my estimation, right up to the time of his death, Brameld was engaged in the process of modifying his philosophy of educational reconstructionism. Brameld devoted a large part of the current book to coming to grips with "developments in philosophical, social, and educational theory which are often uncrystallized and still immature." Among these "developments"—what he referred to as "frontiers"—are logical analysis, creativity, social-self-realization, and evolution. In the following section, I want to comment briefly on three of his other frontiers—sociological realism, existential humanism, and religion—as particular examples of what Brameld called "education's most neglected problem"—*values education*. I especially want to show how remarkably forward-looking, and applicable his thinking on these value issues is for today's schools and colleges.

Values Education

Brameld insisted in *Education as Power* that, because education was a "high profession," then educators needed a drastically revamped training (a seven-year curriculum) that was at least the equivalent of what was available in the best schools of medicine and law. For educators (both teachers and administrators), this would mean an extensive general education in philosophy, literature, history, the arts, and the natural sciences; an in-depth understanding of such behavioral sciences as anthropology, psychology, sociology, economics, and political science; and an intensive year of study in educational theory, particularly philosophy and history of education. Finally, Brameld's revision of teacher preparation would include the "requirement of practice" distributed evenly throughout the preparation program, featuring frequent community service, intense study of all the known "methodologies of teaching and learning," leading to the culminating "seventh-year internship."

Noteworthy here, I believe, is that even though Brameld himself was prepared in an academic field (philosophy at the University of Chicago), and taught for several years in liberal-arts colleges, I never once heard, or read, him disparage the importance of teaching and learning methodologies in professional schools. However, I did occasionally hear him criticize some professors in the disciplines, who in spite of their ridicule of "how-to" educationists, were themselves "atrocious classroom performers...who knew nothing about how to teach." Also significant here is that Brameld's recommendation for a "seven-year" professional preparation curriculum is only now, 35 years later, beginning to catch on as some colleges of education are moving to require 5th and 6th years of post-baccalaureate training for teacher certification *after* the completion of a four-year liberal arts education. As yet, however, few teacher education programs in the

United States have come even close to achieving the spectacular breadth and depth of Brameld's vision for changing teacher education.

The core of Brameld's "normative design for the professional preparation of teachers" was extensive study in the humanities, behavioral sciences, and educational theory, preparation he believed to be the *sine qua non* for teaching about values. How important were values? Here is Brameld at his rhetorical best on the need to "axiologize" education at all levels:

> The time indeed is already well passed when we can afford to indulge in the luxury of cluttered curriculums, in spurious academic aloofness rationalized in the name of objectivity, in confused if not often obsolete codes of moral conduct, and in stultifying ambitions to grasp the dubious goals of success and status at whatever cost to our personal and communal integrity. For the grim truth is that nothing less than the life of mankind as a whole is now in precarious balance. To reassert that values are education's most neglected problem is really to insist that we no longer have any genuine choice but to bring the nature and meaning of values out of the shadowy background and into the spotlight of sustained concern on every level of learning from kindergarten through the university.

For Brameld, axiological questions such as: What should we know? How should we live together? What moral principles should guide our lives? How can we treat each other more humanely? What should we value? What should we believe? And how can we build a more peaceful and just world? must become the heart and soul of schooling at all levels. Furthermore, he maintained that educators must always discuss these questions in an open-ended, rather than an indoctrinative, manner, with the purpose of achieving what he called "consensual validation." This is an open, dialectical, cooperative, searching examination of evidence to support one's reasons for advancing particular preferences, with the ultimate goal of reaching consensus. Without serious training in philosophy and the behavioral sciences, teachers would be unable to handle such complex questions in a professionally competent and mutually respectful way. Brameld believed that these types of questions required a genuine interdisciplinary approach to subject matter that, in my opinion, still remains an elusive, but highly desirable, goal to this day in elementary, secondary, and higher education.

One of Brameld's value "frontiers," *sociological realism*, anticipated the thinking of today's critical theorists by at least two decades. Little did he know that his statement—"So-called impartial truth about human experience does not occur anywhere nearly as often as truth which is colored and formed by one's class orientation"—would set the stage for two decades of probing social and educational analysis by the critical pedagogues of the 1980s and 1990s. In fact, one leading contemporary critical pedagogue, Henry Giroux (1988), refers directly to Brameld's writings as the precursor for much of his own current work. Sociological realism was the term Brameld used to make the point that a conception of truth which was absolute, context-free, and mind-independent was virtually non-existent. Truth is always and everywhere a matter of perspective, usually mediated through one's membership in a particular social class, ethnicity, race, gender, religion, and sexual orientation.

Objective and impartial proclamations of truth *a la* the perennialists and the essentialists, according to Brameld, are often shields for ignoring the conscious and unconscious biases that influence educators' values. For Brameld, the upshot of an understanding of sociological realism was that teachers and administrators had to "understand their class positions in American culture"; that, for example, the control of schools and colleges throughout the United States rested, in large part, in the hands of middle-class elites. Education is never a value-neutral activity, and when educators can understand, and try to transcend, their own class biases, then they can more effectively serve the needs and interests of all students everywhere. Brameld's sociological realism was the 1960s forerunner of a radical, postmodern politics that has affected virtually all the humanities and social sciences in the academy at the present time (see, for example, Steven Seidman, ed., 1994); and, yet, unfortunately, because of its highly controversial political implications, the concept still has not taken hold in America's public schools.

Another of Brameld's value "frontiers," *existential humanism*, spoke to his delicately nuanced understanding that although the dynamic pursuit of real, egalitarian decision-making was a vital part of living and learning in a democracy, life as a whole was not always rational, logical, or susceptible to exact social planning. Neither could it be fully explained by referring to the cultural contingencies of sociological realism. While the sociological realist might agree with the existential humanist that indeed "existence precedes essence"—that is class interests and judgments always come before, and influence, so-called "objective" or rational judgments about the truth of existence—nevertheless, the two departed in a major way. For the existential humanist, according to Brameld, there was a "fundamental, unrational, primordial self" that preceded *all* sociological contingencies, including class interests. Moreover, according to Brameld, the existential humanist was "trying to help us face the truth that there is something dreadful about reality. This dreadfulness centers in the mystery and inevitability of death."

At the present time, of course, a postmodern philosopher like Richard Rorty (1989) would vigorously repudiate the assumption that any self could ever be pre-existent, capable of transcending its context and contingencies, or even that there is anything resembling a "primordial self" that is not socially constructed. He would also say that if there is something "dreadful" about reality, it is only because people have imposed this particular narrative structure on the "blooming, buzzing confusion" that characterizes their lives. Brameld believed otherwise, and postmodernists would do well to hear his message today. Partly in response to those critics who attacked him on the pretext that his philosophy of educational reconstruction was hyper-rationalistic and triumphantly utopian, Brameld set out in *Education as Power* to demonstrate that his educational reconstructionism did indeed possess a tragic sense, a sense of the depth and significance of being despite the stark finitude of human life. Brameld spent some of his later years trying to add a dimension to his educational philosophy that "deepened the meaning of being, the meaning of both subjective and objective reality."

Where Richard Rorty, the critical pedagogues, and other contemporary postmodernists could well benefit from a careful reading of *Education as Power* is in Brameld's insight that there is more to life than simply coming to grips with the impress of our cultural contingencies, or unmasking the reactionary political pretensions of those in power. We live, too, within the imprint of a mystery so vast that, at times, it dwarfs our immediate sociological predicaments. The trouble with postmodernism is that it remains oblivious to the ultimate riddle of what it means to be human. Postmodernism's emphasis is excessively pragmatic, political, presentist, deterministic, and materialistic. Its sense of irony has less to do with confronting the tragic sense of life and more to do with either savoring life's sardonic and implausible qualities or energetically exposing the West's long history of ruthless expansion, exploitation, and oppression. Brameld, especially toward the end of his career, was trying to enlarge his reconstructionist philosophy of education to address what he called life's "unrational" existential factors: alienation, anxiety, inauthenticity, dread, sense of nothingness, and the ever-present anticipation of the finality of death. The lesson for educators today, I am sure Brameld would concur, is to teach students to live courageously and actively in the face of all of life's existential perplexities, recognizing that there is sometimes more to the unfathomable dilemma of human existence than meets the postmodern eye.

Finally, perhaps Brameld's most controversial proposal for rejuvenating the value dimension of schooling in America was for education *to deal openly with religion* at all levels of schooling, in a manner that was neither subservient, dogmatic, nor propagandistic. For Brameld, moral and character education was incomplete if it refused to tackle religious issues head-on. Brameld himself, although acutely aware of the importance of the life of the spirit to human beings everywhere, was a resolute secular humanist. Not for him was the perennialist-essentialist take on religion which held that the "ultimate meaning of life and destiny" resided in some kind of Absolute Being. For the perennialist-essentialist, the purpose of religious studies was to "teach understanding and worship of God."

In contrast, the progressivist-reconstructionist perspective was one that believed human beings—not a God or a Supreme Force—ought to direct the course of their own lives, by making their own rules and laws, while eschewing any supernatural "quest for certainty," to use John Dewey's (1929) phrase. The progressivist-reconstructionist held that if life was to be made better for all peoples, then human beings "needed to build it through [their] own struggles, [their] own aspirations, [their] own scientific and creative powers." In this secular sense, according to Brameld, the Ten Commandments were actually cultural constructions that people shaped out of their experiences, in order to invent a better way to live productively and peacefully with each other. For Brameld, educators who traditionally engaged in the debate around the proper place of religion in American education usually lined up on one or the other side of the perennialist-essentialist/progressivist-reconstructionist divide. Brameld's own preference, based on his belief that education was "primarily modification" rather than "transmission," was to insist that what human beings actually needed was *less* faith in a supernatural creature who supported the status quo and *more* faith in their own powers to upset the status quo in order to create a better world.

Despite his own unapologetic partiality for a scientific or secular humanism, however, Brameld was convinced that human beings would never succeed fully in grasping the meaning of their existence. Even with the remarkable breakthroughs in astronomy, cosmology, and physics, Brameld realized that we still know relatively little about the nature and destiny of the universe. For example, in the 1960s there was "not a shred of direct evidence" that life actually existed on other planets; today the same holds true. And, so, while we possess great scientific power to comprehend and control nature and human nature, there is still an enormous amount that we do not know about the mystery of existence. At this point, we can only continue to investigate its enigmas, while marveling at the variety of religio-spiritual approaches that people have taken since the beginning of time in order to understand and appreciate it.

To this end, in the early 1960s Brameld came up with a thoroughly radical proposal: the schools must allow students to study in depth the "great religious approaches to life and the universe—Oriental, Occidental, humanistic, theistic." And along the way students must also learn that while religions have, throughout human history, been sources of enormous hope in the presence of fear, hatred, and ignorance, they have also failed to deliver fully on their promise to create a world of universal love and compassion. At the present time, a number of prominent educational philosophers (for example, Noddings, 1993; Nord & Haynes, 1998; Sears & Carper, 1998) are just beginning to make a similar case that students need the time and space in schools and colleges to study the great existential and religious questions, but none have said it with more elan than Brameld.

Brameld favored critically robust dialogue on religion: he was insistent that teachers should encourage students to understand, compare, criticize, and argue about the virtues and vices of the greater and lesser religious orientations with one end in view: to arrive "at their own free agreements or disagreements as to which, if any, of the major religious philosophies offers them the most help and the richest promise." The following assertions remain trenchant, and necessary, even today, as experiments to teach about religion in the public schools of America take either an innocuous or a dogmatic form: teaching the bible as benign literature or history, or teaching the bible as The Revealed Word of God.

> Nor do I believe that it is at all improper for education to be imbued with the quality of religiosity—certainly not if one defines that word in such nonsectarian terms as the total devotion of any person to the search for life's highest values. What *is* improper, of course, is any kind of education that allows religiosity to overcome the completely equal requirement of critical and constant readiness to

examine *every* commitment and to correct *every* weakness that such examination may expose.

A Final, Personal Reflection

We shall not cease from exploration
And the end of all our exploring
Will be to arrive where we started
And know the place for the first time.
—T. S. Eliot, *Little Gidding*

Rereading Ted Brameld's *Education as Power* in order to prepare this Foreword poignantly reminded me of the truth of T. S. Eliot's oft-quoted lines from *Little Gidding*. I became acutely aware of the career-long impact Ted has had on my teaching and writing, even though at times in the past, while trying to forge my own intellectual identity and independence, I denied it to myself. Over the years, I had simply forgotten the amazing breadth and depth of this man's influence on me, and of how much, even today, I continue to teach and write in the light of his example. After all my exploring, I have indeed arrived at the place where I started. I am sure that this is true to some degree for the majority of Ted's former students.

For example, in the years following my doctoral studies with Ted, I gradually drifted away from educational reconstructionism's more *political* purposes. I frequently questioned how, or why, I ought to make the creation of a world civilization *the* "galvanizing purpose of public education." I found myself implicitly agreeing with a criticism made by a well-known educational philosopher of the 1960s, J. E. McClellan, that Ted quotes in the current book:

> "I rather think that Mr. Brameld worships the Golden Calf of a 'democratic world community,' mistaking it for God.... We've offended his religion, for we don't advocate an education built around the worship of his (or any other) god. The attitude of critical disciplined intelligence and the attitude of emotional involvement are antithetical."

But in re-examining *Education as Power* from my current vantage point of the year 2000, and in thinking about all that has happened that makes the world a very dangerous place in the intervening years since Ted wrote this book, I know that Professor McClellan was wrong and Ted was right. It is entirely possible, indeed it is crucial, for an educator to possess *both* a "disciplined intelligence" *and* a passionate, "emotional" commitment to politico-educational ideals worth pursuing. One without the other makes the ideals unattainable. In reality, I have not drifted very far from Ted's political ideals after all.

Today I find myself agreeing wholeheartedly with him that, by and large, Americans have been far too ethnocentric in their relationship to the rest of the world. Furthermore, nationalism still remains perhaps the most "imminent force of destruction" civilization has ever known. And racism, anti-Semitism, sexism, homophobia, political self-righteousness, and classism will continue to plague humanity in every corner of the globe unless people make a conscious effort to stop looking for an "other" to hate. What is more, the persecution *of religion*, and the violence perpetrated *in the name of religion*, are mutually self-reinforcing and equally evil, and will end only when human beings stop looking to the heavens for Gods who favor one "tribe" over all the others. Also, as long as the industrialized nations continue to exploit the world's natural resources for no apparent reason than to provide extravagant creature comforts, then the planet's delicate environmental equilibrium will deteriorate beyond restoration, if it has not already. Finally, the worldwide power struggle for market supremacy commodifies, and cheapens, every aspect of human existence, including, most critically, the relational and the spiritual.

It is truly alarming to realize that the crisis state of the world of the early 21st century has actually changed very little from when Ted lived in it—in spite of some major political, scientific, and technological breakthroughs since his death. And, sadly, education remains about as system-maintaining and intellectually hidebound as it ever was, despite some well-publicized curricular and instructional tinkering at the margins. It was while re-reading Ted's book that I was captured yet one more time by his unremitting zeal for world civilization. He understood well, half a century ago, that without some type of international order, without some form of world community, without some persistent, centralized effort on the part of international leaders to locate, affirm, and strengthen the universal values that could bind all civilizations together in mutual peace and productivity, we will never be able to achieve the ultimate safeguard against world war, and avoid the virtual annihilation of the human species that could very well accompany it.

In spite of Ted's prophetic sense of geo-political urgency, however, and contra Professor McClellan, I cannot cite a single sentence in *Education as Power* that presents the ideal of world community as a "golden calf" that Brameld wants all of us to "worship." Instead, I find several passages such as the following:

> As I regard it, the utopian mood never aims at ultimate perfection. Such an aim only invites rigid-minded faith in some form of spurious salvation either in heaven or on earth. I see no contradiction between the requirement of far-reaching cultural portrayals based upon substantial knowledge of all of the sciences and the arts, and the equal requirement of adequate room for radical corrections or additions to these portrayals.

Ted is telling us that educators must be utopian in their aims, but never obdurately so. Blueprints for world community are by their very nature uncertain, always projects in process, and critical corrections must become an ongoing phenomenon. Furthermore, it is essential that, as a transmissive *and* transformative cultural institution, the world's schools and colleges have a pivotal part to play in creating any models for a new world order. In fact, as Ted frequently reminds his readers, America's schools and colleges ought to consider embracing the notion of world civilization as a way to integrate curricula that, for most of the twentieth century, have remained thematically scattered and philosophically rudderless. At the very least, Ted believes that schools and colleges throughout the world ought to encourage students to talk openly and honestly about all the "crisis" issues I mentioned earlier—with the purpose of "finding a common ground, a place on which to stand, not against one another, but with one another."

As I bring this Foreword to a close, and as I reflect back on my three-plus decades of teaching and writing in the academy, I wish to end on a very personal note. At this time, I want to offer publicly both my gratitude and my deepest affection to a mentor I regretfully lost touch with during the latter part of his life. Although I have rarely used Ted Brameld's exact vocabulary, or even referred to him directly, in my teaching and writing, I find I have dealt at length with many of the same issues he did, and from an eerily similar perspective. For example, I realize that in my scholarly work I too have had a career-long penchant for quadruple categories that are roughly analagous to Ted's perennialism, essentialism, progressivism, and reconstructionism. In *Answering the "Virtuecrats"* (1997), I referred to four types of character-education initiatives as "neo-classical," "communitarian," "liberationist," and "postmodern." And in *Faith, Hype, and Clarity* (1999), I designated four religio-spiritual narratives as "fundamentalist," "prophetic," "alternative spiritualities," and "post-theist." And while my *"Real World" Ethics* (1996) presents a typology of what I call "First, Second, and Third Moral Languages," my approach to ethical analysis has Ted's philosophical imprint all over it—still one more example of discovering that I have arrived back at the "home" from whence I started, amidst all my circuitous intellectual explorations.

Each one of my three, aforementioned books is rooted in a stance of progressive liberalism. Better still, using Ted's language, I come out of a "cultural interpretation" that today I would call a "postmodern reconstructionism," a creative reconfiguration of Richard Rorty's neo-pragmatism (1998), Jurgen Habermas's (1987) neo-liberalism, and Ted's social reconstructionism. Rorty aestheticizes and "ironizes" public conversation; Habermas rationalizes and politicizes it; while Brameld democratizes and internationalizes it. So, as well, many of my scholarly articles through the years have promoted a view of education that is transformative rather than transmissive, one that challenges, deconstructs, and looks for more democratic alternatives to established politico-educational arrangements—rather than one that simply accepts, and adapts to, them. Somewhat surprisingly, I discovered while preparing this Foreword that much of what I have written in several of these shorter pieces is highly congruent, not only with the ideas in *Education as Power*, but also with its language and the tone.

Finally, I want Ted to know that I have always been, and I will continue to be, a "values" educator, just as he advocated. I have created and administered an Interdisciplinary graduate program in the helping professions that closely approximates the purposes Ted enunciates in his "charter for educational leadership" in the final pages of *Education as Power*. Like him, I believe we need to ground leadership programs in what he calls "eight guiding concepts": creativity, audacity, directiveness, convergence, commitment, confrontation, involvement, and control. How much more imaginative, activistic, and inspirational are these ideals than the insipid pieties—e.g., competence in management skills, team-building, caring—enumerated in the usual educational leadership catalogues.

Furthermore, as a foundations of education professor, I have developed a number of courses in several disciplines that push students in many human service professions to examine closely, and when necessary to amend, their axiological biases. While some of these courses may not be as overtly political as Ted would like, they would, I think, please him very much. I have spent the last decade of my life in higher education attempting to create both a *modus operandi* and a *modus vivendi* for people in a number of professional venues to communicate respectfully yet candidly with each other across their ideological differences—with the purpose of finding some common philosophical and political ground. I call this process the "moral conversation" (Nash, 1996), and it has been indelibly influenced by concepts I first learned in Ted's courses 35 years ago: defensible partiality, consensual validation, social-self-realization, existential humanism, the power of the unrational, interdisciplinary study, sociological realism, and moral and character education. I can honestly say at this time that my debt to Ted regarding my work on the "moral conversation" is incalculable.

To educators everywhere, I can only assert that *Education as Power* is a penetrating and timely read. I, for one, intend to adopt this re-issue in my philosophy of education course, and the first assignment I will give my students is to write their own Forewords to the book, in light of their current professional circumstances. And to Ted Brameld I can only say *requiescas in pace*, old friend, and thank you for your patience in helping me to arrive, finally, at the place where I started, but in my own way and in my own time.

Bibliography

Ayers, W. & Miller, J.L., editors. (1998). *A light in dark times: Maxine Greene and the unfinished conversation.* New York: Teachers College Press.

Boulding, E. (1998). *Building a global civic culture: Education for an interdependent world.* Syracuse, NY: Syracuse University Press.

Brameld, T. (1947). Philosophies of education in an age of crisis. *School and Society*, 65, 452-460.

Brameld, T. (1971). *Patterns of educational philosophy: Divergence and convergence in culturological perspective.* New York: Holt, Rinehart, & Winston.

Bussler, D., O'Neil, F.L., Raffel, A., Stone, F.A., and Thomas, T.M. (1997). *Introducing educational reconstruction: The philosophy and practice of transforming society through education.* San Francisco, CA: Caddo Gap Press.

Dewey, J. (1960). *The quest for certainty: A study of the relation of knowledge and action.* New York: G. P. Putnam's Sons. (Original work published 1929)

Freire, P. (1985). *The politics of education: Culture, power, and liberation.* South Hadley, MA: Bergin & Garvey.

Giroux, H. (1988). *Schooling and the struggle for public life: Critical pedagogy in the modern age.* Minneapolis, MN: University of Minnesota Press.

Habermas, J. (1987). *The philosophical discourse of modernity.* New York:

Political Press.

Horton, M., with Kohl, J. & Kohl, H. (1990). *The long haul: An autobiography*. New York: Doubleday.

Huntington, S. P. (1996). *The clash of civilizations and the remaking of world order*. New York: Simon & Schuster.

Kohl, H. (1998). *The discipline of hope: Learning from a lifetime of teaching*. New York: Simon & Schuster.

Kozol, J. (1992). *Savage inequalities: Children in America's schools*. New York: Crown.

Kuhn, T. S. (1970). *The structure of scientific revolutions* (2nd ed.). Chicago, IL: University of Chicago Press.

Nash, R. J. (1996). Fostering moral conversations in the college classroom. *Journal on Excellence in College Teaching*, 7, 83-106.

Nash, R. J. (1996). *"Real World" Ethics: Frameworks for educators and human service professionals*. New York: Teachers College Press.

Nash, R. J. (1997). *Answering the "virtuecrats": A moral conversation on character education*. New York: Teachers College Press.

Nash, R. J. (1999). *Faith, hype, and clarity: Teaching about religion in American schools and colleges*. New York: Teachers College Press.

Noddings, N. (1993). *Educating for intelligent belief or unbelief*. New York: Teachers College Press.

Nord, W. A. & Haynes, C. C. (1998). *Taking religion seriously across the curriculum*. Alexandria, VA: Association for Supervision and Curriculum Development.

Rorty, R. (1989). *Contingency, irony, and solidarity*. New York: Cambridge University Press.

Rorty, R. (1998). *Achieving our country: Leftist thought in twentieth-century America*. Cambridge, MA: Harvard University Press.

Sears, J. T. & Carper, J. C. (Eds.). (1998). *Curriculum, religion, and public education: Conversations for an enlarging public square*. New York: Teachers College Press.

Seidman, S. (Ed.). (1994). *The postmodern turn: New perspectives on social theory*. New York: Cambridge University Press.

Thomas, T.M., Conrad, D.R., & Langsam, G.F., editors. (1987). *Global images of peace and education: Transforming the war system*. Ann Arbor, MI: Prakken Publications.

Selected Works of Theodore Brameld

Brameld, T. (1946). *Minority problems in the public schools.* New York: Harper & Row.

Brameld, T. (1951). The philosophy of reconstructionism. *Educational Theory*, August.

Brameld, T. (1952). Causation, goals, and methodology. *Educational Theory*, July.

Brameld, T. (1956). *Toward a reconstructed philosophy of education.* New York: Holt, Rinehart & Winston.

Brameld, T. (1957). *Cultural foundations of education.* New York: Harper & Row.

Brameld, T. (1959). *The remaking of a culture: Life and education in Puerto Rico.* New York: Harper & Row.

Brameld, T. (1965). *Education for the emerging age.* New York: Harper & Row.

Brameld, T. (1965). *Education as power.* New York: Holt, Rinehart, & Winston.

Brameld, T. (1965). *The use of explosive ideas in education.* Pittsburgh, PA: The University of Pittsburg Press.

Brameld, T. (1966). Reconstructionist theory: Some recent critiques considered in perspective. *Educational Theory*, October.

Brameld, T. (Ed.) (1967). Learning through involvement: Puerto Rico as a laboratory in educational anthropology. *Journal of Education*, December.

Brameld, T. (1968). *Japan: Culture, education, and change in two communities.* New York: Holt, Rinehart & Winston.

Brameld, T. (1970). *The climactic decades: Mandate to education.* New York: Praeger.

Brameld, T. (1970). A cross-cutting approach to the curriculum: The moving wheel. *Phi Delta Kappan*, March.

Brameld, T. (1971). *Patterns of educational philosophy: Divergence and convergence in culturological perspective.* New York: Holt, Rinehart & Winston.

Brameld, T. (1974). Culturology as the search for convergence. In P.A. Bertocci, editor, *Mid-twentieth century American philosophy.* New York: Humanities Press.

Brameld, T. (1976). *The teacher as world citizen.* Homewood, IL: ETC Publications.

Brameld, T. (1977). Reconstructionism as a radical philosophy of education: A reappraisal. *The Educational Forum, 42*, November, 67-76.

Brameld, T. (1977). Social frontiers, retrospective and prospective. *Phi Delta Kappan, 59* (2), October, 118-120.

Brameld, T., with Matsuyama, M. (1977). *Tourism as cultural learning*. Lanham, MD: University Press of America.

Original Preface

The thorny problems of education that are debated and redebated in the present period of our history are are much too frequently viewed in exclusively American terms. The truth is that they are by no means exclusively Ameican. Far more often they turn out to be problems of planet-wide scope. One principal reason, indeed, why American education so often proves inept in clarifying them succinctly or in acting upon them concertedly is that they are treated in the provincial perspective that still remains characteristic of typical American attitudes toward man and society.

I shall demonstrate in these pages that educational issues of the most urgent concern are often at least as distressing to another and far distant culture as they are to our own. Similarly, although the audiences with which my ideas were first shared consisted chiefly of teachers, professors, and other educators living in Korea, halfway around the globe, what I said to them could just as appropriately have been said in any average American community. Only one important difference exists between the two audiences: in Korea, I felt repeatedly that my listeners were understanding what I was saying more sensitively and accurately than would many American listeners. And this despite the fact that every sentence had to be translated on the spot into the native language.

Why did my Korean friends understand me more clearly? Because, I believe, the matters of which I spoke are more poignantly disturbing to a people that has known directly and terribly the meaning of our age of upheaval than to a people whose concern with that meaning is more often likely to be feeble and superficial. To talk with Korean citizens forthrightly of the issues considered in this book is to cut deeply into their own recent, bitter experience. Education *as* power is a theme that makes sense to people who know firsthand that life today cannot be understood except in terms of the struggle *for* power.

This is by no means to suggest that Americans are unwilling to respond to these issues, once presented to their attention. My experience with teachers, students, and parents in many sections of our country convinces me that, if they are given the opportunity, they are entirely willing, even anxious, to respond. The difficulty is that too rarely are they afforded this kind of opportunity. The dominant concerns of most educational spokesmen today are not usually those which I discuss in these chapters. They are concerns of emergency means much more than long-range ends. They are concerns of a practical and instrumental nature: programed instruction is a conspicuous example. The voices of audacity and creative excitement that characterized American educational theory a quarter of a century or more ago are now muted voices. Most of our younger philosophers of education are preoccupiedwith matters that strike as little spark and have as little impact upon educational adventure as contemporary American philosophy in general has upon American life.

Let me reiterate my conviction, however, that Americans deeply concerned about education are as quick to respond to issues of ends as they are to issues of means, to far-reaching goals as to pedestrian tasks. My confidence in this potential readiness among American citizens has been confirmed as I have come to know and admire many Asian citizens. For, as innumerable travelers to distant lands have discovered, the basic needs and hopes of mankind are far more alike than they are different. The average Japanese desires health and peace as much as the average European. The average Latin American desires respect and dignity as much as the average Australian. The average Korean desires good education as much as the average American.

The most recent opportunity I have had to reinforce these beliefs was made possible by an invitation from the U. S. Department of State to lecture in Japan and Korea on questions of American education and civilization. The Korean lectures were arranged in part also through the Fulbrighit Commission. I am especially indebted to Dr. Hyan Ki Paik, Director of the Central Education Institute of Korea, to Mr. Jong-Gon Hwang of the Research Institute staff, and to Mr. Chung-do Ihm, recently of the U. S. Embassy staff in Korea, for their many efforts in my behalf.

With the exception of the last two chapters, the lectures are reproduced essentially in the form of their original presentation. I have wanted to preserve as far as possible their rather conversational, nontechnical style and tone. My hope in doing this has been that Americans interested in the cutting-edges of educational theory will thereby more easily become aquainted with my viewpoint than they might by turning to my more elaborate professional works. I realize, of course, that this form of presentation is bound at times to oversimplify and overgeneralize. Readers are therefore invited to consult my other works for refinements of evidence and argument. At the same time, it should be noted that most of the chapters an this book develop ideas that have not hitherto received my attention in comparable ways. Chapter 3, "Conflicts in American Educational Theory," will be most familiar to students of my position, whereas Chapter 8,"The Religious Dimension of Education," may be least so. The two concluding chapters on "Values" and "World Civilization," although presented in the Korean series, were originally prepared in somewhat expanded form for two national conferences of Phi Delta Kappa, the American educational fraternity. They are reproduced essentially in that form with the generous permission of Phi Delta Kappa.

With equally generous permission, I also include as an appendix a lecture presented before the conference titled "Educational Administration—Philosophy in Action," to which I was invited by the Ninth University Council for Educational Administration Career Development Seminar, Oklahoma Center for Continuing Education, University of Oklahoma. This lecture tries to epitomize for an American audience of educational leaders a number of the theses treated in the lectures. To the degree that it succeeds in doing so, it reinforces my opening contentions that the problems facing our time transcend national boundaries and provincial attitudes because they are to be found everywhere that human beings engage in teaching and learning. And this means, of course, almost everywhere on earth.

I am deeply obligated to all those in the U. S. Department of State, in Asia, and in American universities, who made this book possible. Particularly, as a citizen of the United States, I wish to express my pride in the right of minority dissent—a citizen who can, if he so wishes, disagree with prevailing majority opinion and with official foreign policy, yet realize that he is respected and encouraged in his right to do so.

—Theodore Brameld
Boston University
February 1965

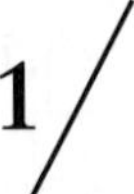

Education as Power

"Education as power" is truly an explosive theme. This is indeed an age of power. It is the first age in which man has learned how to release the energies of physical and chemical nature in such a way as to enable him, either to remake his world in a new and wonderful image of technological and esthetic achievement, or to commit mass suicide.

This is an age of power. The question that we have not yet confronted, however, is whether education shares in this power, and if so whether it is merely the servant of other kinds of power or is also a generator and director of power. Discussion of education today has very little meaning except in the setting of world crisis. My contention is that if education is to become meaningful in such a setting, it too must become powerful. It is, in fact, the one power left in the world that is greater than the forces of nature that man has now enslaved. Only the power of education is capable of controlling the other powers that man has gained and will use either for his annihilation or for his transformation.

The idea of education as power is not a new one. Indeed, a very great man stated it far better nearly four centuries ago than anyone has ever done since—the English philosopher Francis Bacon. "Knowledge is power," he declared. In a sense, this is my thesis also.

But there are certain difficulties in the Baconian dictum. A moment's thought reveals that the key words, actually, stand for amoral concepts. Power, as such, is neither moral nor immoral. It is morally neutral and consequently amoral. That is to say, power can be used either for evil purposes or for good purposes. A power machine such as a tractor or a rocket is indifferent to how you use it. You can use the tractor to destroy a paddy of rice or to produce food for hungry people; you can use the rocket to blow up cities or to improve communication by satellite.

But so, too, is knowledge amoral. Per se, it can be exploited either for horribly destructive or for beautifully constructive ends. The scientific knowledge which has produced nuclear energy is itself amoral knowledge. The scientists who invented and learned to control the atom were in so doing amoral scientists. They did not directly concern themselves with the question of whether nuclear energy would become a monstrous evil or a magnificent good.

In short, power as such is amoral and knowledge as such is amoral. The crucial problem of our time is how to assure that both power and knowledge will be developed and applied neither for amorality nor immorality, but for utmost morality.

You see how quickly, when we start examining familiar terms, we must turn to philosophy for help. For in one sense philosophy, as I shall later consider more fully, is the discipline which gives clarity of meaning to the symbols we use. The question that now arises, then, is this: What do the philosophers of education, at least in the United States, think about the problem of knowledge as power? Do they agree with Francis Bacon? Do they disagree? And if they agree, how do they propose to channel the power of knowledge for good purposes rather than for bad purposes?

American philosophers of education disagree with one another a great deal. Nevertheless, there are three areas of consensus on the question before us. First, undoubtedly the most influential theorists agree that in some respects knowledge is power. But, second, they also at once agree that education thus far has not learned how to develop sufficient power to guarantee control over the powers that science and technology release. In this sense, they would say that education is guilty of a tragic lag: it is not keeping up with the fundamental revolutions that are consequent upon the discovery and control of the energies of nature. Hence a wide gap exists between education as power, on the one side, and science as power, on the other side. Third, they more or less agree, I think, that we must find a way to ensure that the power of education becomes superior to any other power. For the alternative may be that we shall be destroyed as a human race.

Philosophic positions: education as power

Let us now consider the different philosophic answers educators give to the question: How can education become powerful enough? In doing so, let us assume further that at least four major trends or points of view now prevail in educational theory in the United States. These trends will also receive attention later on, so do not be too much disturbed if my preliminary characterizations seem inadequate. They are indeed inadequate. Even so, they will, I hope, both serve our present purpose and prepare the ground for what is to follow.

The first point of view takes the position, broadly stated, that the best possible policy that the schools and colleges can now adopt is to enroll in the power struggle within and among nations, in order to support America and her allies in their efforts to become supreme over both internal and external challengers. This can only mean that the schools must be harnessed to the power structure of American politics and American economics. Hence a central rcsponsibility of education becomes that of discovering and preparing the minority of superior students who can become the engineers or other experts required to assure American superiority in such areas as the race for nuclear domination and the conquest of space.

Training in mathematics, physics, and other disciplines necessary to technological and military power thus takes priority over all other educational activities. At the same time, this first general viewpoint readily concedes that the average student must be educated to the limits of his ability—above all, his ability both to understand and serve the prevailing power struggle on his own level, and to accept the moral precept that it is right to support and wrong to oppose "our side" of that struggle. Repeatedly in the past few years, American education has been urged, sometimes subtly and sometimes obtrusively, to enlist its energies in behalf of the dominant power structure, and therefore in behalf of the kinds of knowledge and the competencies that will assure victory in competition with allegedly hostile power structures.

The second point of view appears to be very different from the first. It holds that if knowledge is power the foremost task of education is to develop the power that lies in reason, and in the capacity to acquire knowledge based solely upon reason. It denies that education should be directly involved in the power struggle of nations. On the contrary, it holds that education can be helpful in that struggle only by rising above it—in a sense, by ignoring it. For this position is highly intellectualistic. It contends that education, particularly higher education, should concentrate primarily upon the building of the so-called mental faculties. Only as and if the mental faculties latent in man are developed to their maximum can we be sure that man will use the power of education for good rather than for bad purposes.

Thus the fountainhead of our second viewpoint is Socrates' dictum, "Knowledge is virtue," much more than it is Bacon's dictum, "Knowledge is power." The Socratic position, developed more deeply by Plato and Aristotle, is that only the purest possible knowledge can assure truth, beauty, and goodness, or can demonstrate that all three are ultimately the same. And yet, no matter how difficult it is to attain, here is the one hope for our own age, just as it was the one hope for ancient Greek civilization. The Greeks failed because they did not learn in time that power will corrupt and destroy unless it is exercised by virtuous means for the virtuous ends that reason alone guarantees. So, too, unless we learn in time, will our civilization fail.

Superficially, the third general viewpoint holds with the second that the best way to develop education as power is to teach people how to reason. Nevertheless, it sharply differs with the second as to the nature of reasoning, preferring the term "thinking" and proceeding from quite different psychological assumptions as to what thinking means. In short, the third position contends that the foremost task of education is to develop man's capacity not only to solve problems scientifically, which is in essence the capacity for thinking, but especially to solve problems about himself as well as about the rest of nature.

Thus the third position pivots around one proposition. We have learned how to use the scientific method in mastering the nonhuman world, but we have not really learned how to use it in mastering the human world. We know much less about the psyche scientifically than we do about almost any other phenomenon of nature. We are able to control the atom. We are able to reach farther and farther toward the stars. We are slowly but surely subjugating biological nature—disease, subnormality, and even the death rate. Yet we know very little of how to control our own passions, our anxieties, our fears, or the conflicts both within ourselves as individuals and among ourselves as members of groups, classes, and nations. The third position aims to correct this imbalance by universalizing scientific, reflective thinking throughout education.

In turning finally to the fourth point of view, I should make clear that considerable fault might be found with each of the first three. Some of the difficulties they raise will become apparent further on. At this point, let me merely confess my own preference for the fourth position and introduce it with comparable superficiality.

To begin with, this position is very much concerned with the amoral, immoral, and moral nature of knowledge and power. It holds with all three of the preceding positions that education is compelled to ask and to answer how men can make knowledge as power moral knowledge—that is, how education can be directed through good means and toward good ends. More relentlessly, however, than the other philosophies of education, it asks the question: What is the nature of these good ends toward which education as both good and powerful means should now be directed?

The answer is so imperative that it becomes, as it were, the keystone of the educational arch which these chapters in a sketchy way aim to design. I may only assert here that one moral end takes precedence before all the others to which education should now be dedicated. This is the building of a world order of nations under the direction of the majority of peoples.

The majority of peoples should, through their freely chosen representatives, control all fundamental economic, political, and social policies, and they should do so on a planetary scale. This is the supreme goal of education for the current decades. As long as our schools avoid recognition of this purpose; as long as teachers and professors skirt the subject because it is controversial; as long as educational theorists say, "Oh, no, we must be concerned with training mental faculties," or "We must support the power struggle to glorious victory for our side"—then they are, in my view, denying the central purpose of education. To find a way to enlist and unite the majority of peoples of all races, religions, and nationalities into a great democratic world body with power and authority to enforce its policies—what greater mandate to us in the profession of education can be imagined than this?

The means toward education as power

The question of ends has been stressed first rather than the question of means. This is deliberate. We cannot answer the question of what moral means must be developed in order that education may be more powerful than any other agency on earth, unless we answer the question of the primary moral end for which these means shall be utilized. But if we are clear as to the form and substance of the moral end—the end of a world democratic civilization—then we can turn to the companion question: By what moral means may we achieve such a tremendous moral end?

Here an almost infinite range of largely untapped educational resources is available to us. Let me mention just one resource advocated also by the third position: the power of scientific intelligence ready to be released in attacking the problems of men. Is it not ironical that we know more about how to control the nucleus of hydrogen than we know about how to control the nucleus of human emotion—the libido? Is it not ironical that we know more about how to send astronauts around the earth than we know about how to reduce conflict between groups, much less between nations? One of the fundamental means, therefore, for the achievement of our ends is that of learning how to attack personal and cultural problems with the same scientific intelligence that we use to attack chemical or geological problems. At this point the third and fourth positions are in very close alliance.

I have stated that most of us in education still have to learn how to direct intelligence to the amelioration of human troubles. I should be inaccurate, however, if I contended that this fact is the key to the question of education as power. Basic weaknesses emerge in the third position when it is considered as the sufficient answer. One of these weaknesses lies in the inadequacy of its moral means for the achievement of moral ends. For example, the third position, as it appears to me, underemphasizes the importance of group intelligence expressed in militant collective action—action on the part of people strongly united in behalf of the needed collective ends. More concretely in terms of schools, a still largely undeveloped opportunity exists to teach students of widely varying ages how to work cooperatively and collectively in coping with genuine community problems. These problems should enable students to experience real hurdles in the path of community action. Thereby they may grow into citizens who know how to develop and practice strategies for overcoming them.

The third position does not necessarily deny this kind of experience. On the contrary it often encourages the application of scientific intelligence to stubborn group problems. For the most part, however, it has not emphasized such problems nearly as much as those centering in individual or, at most, small-group behavior. It has much less often focused attention upon the gigantic problems of class or national conflicts. Therefore, in considering the necessity of collective programs of action that come to grips with the power struggle within or among nations, it seems to be cautiously tentative, sometimes evasive, and often hesitant. This weakness is partly due, in turn, to a comparable hesitancy and evasiveness with regard to strong commitment to urgent moral ends—particularly to the clearcut end of a world democratic order of nations.

While much more will have to be said about the fourth position, let me say now that if its full implications were understood it would mean, I am convinced, a revolution in the organization and policies of schools not only of the United States but of many countries. Among other things, it would mean that a substantial part of our tradition-encrusted curricula would have to be discarded. It would mean that our conventional administrative structures would be seen to be often immoral because they are autocratic rather than democratic—not at all geared, accordingly, to teaching teachers and students by experience what education comes to mean when it is powerfully moral both in tactics and in goals. It would mean a much more realistic diagnosis and prognosis of the power structures and struggles of our time, and thus of the obstacles in the way of achieving a peaceful, abundant, and democratic world.

One concluding point. In the United States, most teachers find themselves, willingly and consciously or not, moving in one direction or another with regard to the question of education as power. They may accept the view that the schools and colleges are primarily agents to carry out the orders of the power constellations that are already heavily entrenched in controlling economic, political, and military policies. In this case, they consider their primary obligation to be one of allegiance to those policies. Or, they may accept the alternative view that the basic purpose of education is to teach young people how to become their own masters in practice as well as in theory—in short, to take control of the local, national, and international community rather than to let the community take control of them.

The latter alternative is, of course, implied especially in the fourth position. This position, which I invite you to consider seriously if only to reject finally, is that education as power means first of all education as an agency for the building of a democratic world community. Education as power means that education is the one generative human force potentially great enough to combat all degenerative human forces. Education as power means that we, the teachers, the students, and the parents, are the only ones who should control education—control it for our own good ends and by our own good means.

I am not sure what proportion of American teachers cherish the former view deep in their hearts, and what proportion cherish the latter. I am sure that if education is to become a power mighty enough to control the monstrously immoral forces let loose by the amoral genius of modern physical science, we in education will have to make the second—the only ultimately moral—choice. Education as power means education competent and strong enough to enable us, the majority of people, to decide what kind of a world we want and how to achieve that kind of world. It does not mean education so incompetent and so weak as to let minorities with more power than ourselves make this decision for us.

2/

Crisis as Education

Philosophy, the discipline I represent, has many definitions in the history of scholarship. I would like to select as appropriate to our interest here a definition that has been popular in the last few years, especially in America and England. Philosophy is the examination of the meaning of the language we use; the aim of our examination is to make certain that a particular word means what we presume it to mean. I shall take this definition of philosophy as a starting point and define two further terms necessary to our common understanding—terms left too vague in the opening chapter.

What do we mean by the word crisis? And what is education? These are familiar words. What do we mean when we use them?

A definition of terms

Let us begin with crisis. I submit for your critical consideration the following: crisis connotes a major dislocation—a dislocation of the fundamental institutions, habits, practices, attitudes of any given culture or any section of a culture. When a point is reached in which the major functions, the major structures, the major purposes of a culture or subculture are thrown out of joint, then its members often find themselves bewildered, lost, uprooted. They and their culture are in a state of crisis. A turning point in their history has been reached.

By this definition, few thoughtful persons would care to deny that we live today at such a turning point. Only too grimly is it true that the end of mankind could occur within the lifetime of every one of us. Yet we live also in an age of unprecedented promise. Opportunities for health, for high standards of living, for education are more abundant than at any time in man's entire evolution. The supreme paradox of our age is that in the second half of the twentieth century we possess diametrically contrasting powers at the same moment. On the one hand, we have the power to destroy ourselves at one blow; on the other hand, we have the equally great power to rebuild civilization to a magnificent level of humaneness, of greatness, and of richness. Ours is truly a dislocated time.

A great deal more, of course, could be said to elaborate the meaning of crisis, but remember that at this point we are merely considering preliminary definitions. Let us then leave the term crisis for a moment and turn to the second fundamental term—*education*.

As I hinted in the first lecture, a good deal of disagreement exists, at least in America, over what education means. This is healthy, for it suggests that we may be thinking anew about what we are doing. I suspect, too, that part of our disagreement over what education means is an effect of the current crisis. In times like ours, people tend to reexamine meanings more critically, more searchingly, than in stable times.

Now, as we found in speaking of the word crisis, it is possible to present several different definitions of education and argue about each. The definition of crisis which I asked you to consider already presupposes something of a point of view; so it is with education.

Perhaps most essential is the realization that education is only in small degree an affair of formal institutions set up for the specific purpose of teaching and learning. To understand education in its full scope, we need to perceive it in terms of the role that it plays in the organized life of people. This role is an element of every culture, whether schools as such exist or not. Education is a universal phenomenon; it exists whenever two or more people live together in any kind of organized fashion. Some cultures maintain formal schools, but in certain other cultures, such as the so-called primitive cultures of Australia or Africa, there are no distinctive institutions where the educative process takes place.

What is that process? I suggest that it centers in the necessity for all kinds of human groups to learn how to transmit and how to modify the patterns, the habits and practices, the traditions and skills, that have accumulated as these organized groups have formed themselves into cultures.

To understand the universality of the educative process, let us turn to anthropologists for help. They tell us, first of all, that every culture is entirely learned; it is not, in any sense, inherited through the genetic structure. Language, of course, is a beautiful example of this. All of us have inherited the genetic capacity to speak, to write, to hear a language. But we do not in any sense whatever inherit the capacity to speak, to write, or to read a particular language. This we learn. We learn from the culture, from the "teachers" of the culture, who are first of all our fathers and mothers, or medicine men, or community leaders. And so we learn our culture from infancy by a process of acquisition that is universal to man. As we grow into adults we are thus able to carry on the practices, habits, traditions, customs, and skills which our culture has gradually developed through long periods of history.

Meanwhile, as we learn to transmit the culture to others, we equally learn how to modify it. We learn how to effect gradual or sometimes even quite abrupt changes in the habits, skills, and customs we have acquired. We never merely transmit the same cultural process we have acquired from preceding generations. Always, in some slight degree at least, we modify through our ability to improve upon older ways, to meet new problems and conflicts.

Remember, then, that the educative process seen in the anthropological context of organized ways of life is invariably a bipolar process, or, I should better say, a complementary process. On the one hand, it is a process of stabilizing, of transmitting, of guaranteeing continuity to the culture. On the other hand, it is a process of correcting, improving, and altering the acquired characteristics of past generations.

The role of education in crisis

Now we can place the definitions of crisis and education together. In a time of crisis—that is to say, in a time when the major parts of a culture find themselves in a state of acute dislocation, with all the accompanying conflicts, destructions, and bewilderments that inevitably occur when there is such dislocation—in such a time as this, education invariably reflects the mood of the culture. It does so in ways that would not be equally evident in a time of relative stability, harmony, equilibrium, or balance.

Thus, when crisis occurs, the second of the two major roles of education, the role of modifying, of innovating, becomes stronger. There is greater concern with the causes and corrections of the dislocations that are chronic to crisis. Simultaneously, education becomes both more diagnostic and prognostic, in ways that remind us of medicine as it becomes involved in the diagnosis and prognosis of a disease. A crisis is a time when, as it were, the body politic becomes diseased. Education then becomes concerned with its therapeutic functions to a much greater degree than in normal times.

I should grossly distort the truth, however, to say that at a moment of crisis the schools and other agencies of education suddenly shift to their modifying rather than their transmitting role. This is not what happens. At such a moment, education, like the rest of the culture of which it is an important part, becomes reflective of the bewilderments and confusions that are typical of the culture as a whole.

Then also, teachers, who are the professional representatives of education (I am now speaking of cultures where there are formal schools) begin to reveal in their behavior the uncertainties and conflicts that are everywhere prevalent. By no means do they unite and cry with one voice, "Ah, now our task is perfectly clear. We must perform the modifying role, the therapeutic role, the prognostic role."

Some teachers do so, yes. But many other teachers rush to support the stabilizing role of education even more energetically than in normal times. They are likely to say: "There really isn't any serious crisis. All that we need is more stability and respect for established ways. Schools must perform their traditional roles better than usual by making sure that children are taught the rules, skills, laws, and customs of our culture. Only thus can we assure the stability and security that we once had and must find again."

What actually happens to education in times of crisis is not, then, that all the teachers and other representatives of education join forces. Rather, they tend to fall into opposing camps. They polarize. Some favor a kind of education which strongly supports a modifying role; others tend to become more conservative, more traditional, than ever. So there is within education itself a state of conflict that is symptomatic of the condition of the wider culture.

Let us turn to another way of viewing our problem. It is true that America is not very crisis-minded. Unfortunately, from my viewpoint, large numbers of American citizens would be chagrined to be told that they are living in the midst of crisis. Never having been invaded by a foreign enemy, never having been defeated in a world war, we Americans tend to be complacent and to think that, after all, we are pretty secure, if not even invincible. Perhaps I should use a stronger word than complacent; we are—smug. We tend to be smug because we have never suffered from the great convulsions of the twentieth century as terribly as many other nations have suffered.

This smugness or complacency, however, is a veneer and an illusion. Below the surface of American culture, a tremendous amount of evidence may be found that our country is inextricably involved in the world-wide crisis of our age. Even though many Americans may deny it to themselves, we too, are threatened by catastrophes that could just as easily destroy us, along with the rest of the world, as they could reconstruct us along with the rest of the world.

Education in the culture: a model

Here is a simple model or diagram to help us look at the American culture as a whole. Indeed, if we define culture in terms of the organized patterns of living, you may find here one way to view many cultures of our time.

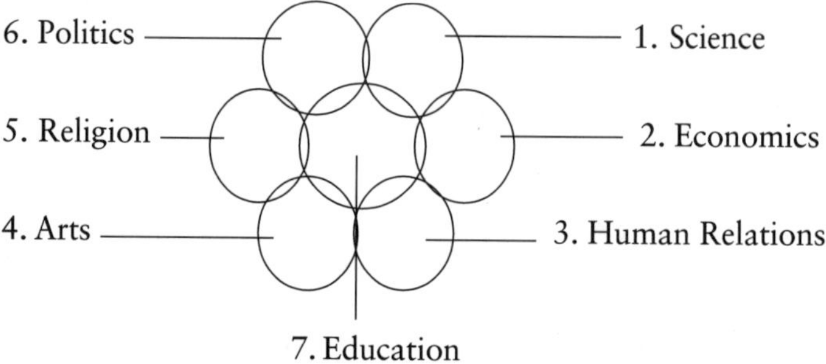

You recognize seven areas of American culture. All overlap, but they are integrated primarily by education. One thing wrong with this little model is that it appears to be static. Actually, no such thing as a static culture can be found anywhere on earth. So I would like to think of our model as moving very rapidly in time from one point to another. Every one of these seven areas of American culture—the area of science, the area of art, the area of religion, the area of human relations, the area of economics, the area of politics, and last but not least, the area of education itself—is beset with conflicts. Each one is suffering from tension between forces that tend to stabilize traditional pattens, and forces that tend to move toward more or less drastic modification of those patterns.

We have space for but one or two illustrations from each area.

Subsequently, a little more evidence will be presented to support some of the generalizations to be offered now.

Take, first, the area of science. I start with it because everyone knows that ours is an age of science. Everyone knows, too, that science is in some ways responsible for the crisis of our age. It is science that has produced our frightful new weapons of destruction. These would not exist without the revolution in physics which we commonly associate with Einstein's theory of relativity.

The example that I choose in the area of science is the painful dilemma that the conscientious scientist now faces. When, on the one hand, he feels compelled to act purely as a scientist, he pursues the objective of truth, indifferent to the moral consequences of his discoveries. To recall an earlier term, he is amoral. On the other hand, he nevertheless realizes that his discoveries do often have profound moral consequences.

In the United States, one certainly can say that never before have so many able scientists suffered so much deep anguish over the problem of moral responsibility as at the present time. Especially is this true among atomic physicists responsible for the invention of the atomic bomb, the hydrogen bomb, and now the cobalt bomb. Some scientists have even been leaders in the struggle to prevent further atomic testing. One of these is the winner of the Nobel Prize in physics, Linus Pauling of the California Institute of Technology.[1] Professor Pauling has devoted much of his time in the last five or more years to fighting atomic testing, chiefly on the ground of its destructive genetic effects. The problem of moral conflict in science generated by the genius of amoral science is my first illustration of the fact of crisis in American culture.

Let us consider an example now from the second area, economics. Here I choose automation, which immediately calls to mind the close relationship between the first and second areas. The marriage of economics and science produces the offspring, technology. And it is technology that has produced, in turn, the phenomenon called automation.

The most thoughtful students of contemporary economics increasingly agree that the growth of the automatized factory is already at a stage of crisis in America. The problem of the displaced worker, the worker no longer needed because the switch button does the job better, inevitably generates greater and greater dislocations in the labor force. How can we keep people employed when the factories are automated to the extent that two or three men perform the work that a hundred or even a thousaud men performed only five or six years ago?

The third area, human relations, is also a very big one. It extends all the way from the individual human being in his relationship to himself to vast groups of people, such as races, religions, and classes. Much time could be spent in illustrating the phenomena of crisis at work in the field of human relations. I select just one phenomenon because it has been dramatized around the world—the conflict in the relations of the Negro and white races in America. In my months abroad, I have had many people ask me about the Negro problem. "Why," they ask, "do you permit the Negro to be treated as he is, especially in the South?" True, some recent improvement in Negro and white relations has occurred in America. But it could also be argued that our race relations are, in some respects, more acutely dislocated now than at any time since the Civil War.

In the area of the arts, it is no less impossible to characterize the situation in a paragraph. Yet the arts in America, as in other countries, are a barometer of the climate of the culture as a whole. The artist, if he is worthy of the name at all, sensitively interprets the times he lives in, and it is not surprising therefore that American art today is in various respects symptomatic of the current time of crisis. Consider as an instance one of the most conspicuous playwrights in America today, Tennessee Williams. His greatest plays deal with the theme of decadence—they portray the human being as sick emotionally, without roots, with little direction or purpose. It is true that one or two of Williams' plays express different themes, but in general his art reflects an anguished and alienated spirit. It is also significant that his plays are more successful than those of any other playwright since Eugene O'Neill, who, by the way, anticipated several of Williams' themes.

In the area of religion, one of the most interesting observations is that the membership of churches in America is growing today proportionally faster than the population as a whole. And yet a number of recent studies show that many people are now joining churches, not primarily because they seek spiritual inspiration, but because membership helps them to move upward in class status, to attain recognition and approval by other members of the community. Thus you find in the American culture today the curious phenomenon of increasing church membership for decreasingly religious reasons. This in itself is surely indicative of extraordinary confusion as to the role that religion plays and should play in American life.

The area of politics is placed next to last, not because it is the least important, but because it may be the most important, or at any rate the most climactic, of the six areas united by education. The example I select to indicate the fact of crisis in American political life is the conflict between those who favor a strongly nationalistic policy and those who favor a strongly international role. This is nothing new. The conflict between nationalism and internationalism is in some respects a very ancient conflict. Yet we can fairly argue that as a result of American participation in two world wars, and as a result of the cold war with the communist bloc, tension between these polarities is becoming more and more severe.

The consequence is that millions of American citizens find themselves in a state of uncertainty as to the meaning of loyalty. Should it be confined to their own nation? Or, in the face of the necessity for a strong international order, should loyalty be extended to a union of nations? This ambivalance is, I submit, unresolved in the average American mind.

A concluding word with regard to the central circle in the diagram: education. Perhaps we have a somewhat clearer idea now of the meaning of my earlier reference to education as the great transmitting and modifying agency of culture. Please notice that the six circles overlap education as well as each other. This means that education is fundamentally concerned in some form or other with each of these six areas. It transmits each, and it is also involved in modifying each.

One of the ways in which one might test the power of education is to ask: To what extent is education in my country involved in the crisis in science? To what extent is it involved in the crisis in economics, in human relations, in the arts, in religion, and in politics?

Indeed, we may evaluate the efficacy of education in any country by asking these questions, and especially by inquiring how successfully it is performing not only its transmitting role but its modifying role as well. Is education helping people to understand the disequilibriums chronic in each of these areas? Is it involved in helping people, who are after all the real substance of education, both to diagnose these disequilibriums and to search for prognoses of personal and collective action by which new equilibriums may be achieved?

Note

[1] In 1963, he also won the Nobel Peace Prize.

3/ *Conflicts in American Educational Theory*

The conflicts in contemporary American educational theory are complicated. It may be helpful to approach them by recalling major points of Chapter 2.

Education today can be understood only in the context of a world-wide crisis—a crisis which in important ways is unique. Certainly it is the most fearful one of all history in that it is capable of producing the most dire consequence to humanity that is conceivable: the end of humanity itself.

Let us recall our definition of crisis. It is not to be understood merely in negative terms. A crisis is a major dislocation of institutions, habits, methods of living, skills, and values. But dislocation also challenges man to seek ways by which a new equilibrium may be established. A crisis is always characterized by both danger and promise.

The history of crisis demonstrates, however, that man has by no means always resolved his crises to his own advantage. Many civilizations have collapsed, as Arnold Toynbee among others has demonstrated. They have collapsed because they were incapable of resolving their crises in favor of a reconstructed and higher equilibrium. But, as Toynbee also contends, this gloomy outcome need not occur.

Thus far, my discussion has been deficient in not explicitly indicating that a crisis in any given culture is also characterized, in a sense, by far-reaching dislocations in the value orientation which had hitherto characterized that culture. Certainly the present crisis is, in a fundamental way, also a crisis in the value orientations of both Western and Eastern civilizations. The old ways of believing in the good life as they regarded it are no longer adequate. Consequently men become deeply disturbed, confused, indeed often emotionally ill, because the value orientation to which they have been accustomed is torn from under them. Thus men seek for some way out, either by returning to some traditional value orientation or perhaps by seeking for some new one.

One may contend that the present crisis in world civilization will not be resolved unless it is possible for humanity to rebuild the traditional value orientations of modern life. I believe that this can be done and that there is a good deal of vital support for such rebuilding. In the chapters to follow, the kind of value orientation I am talking about will become clearer. At the momcnt, I need only express my agreement with the view that crisis is always characterized by a more or less complete breakdown of habitual value orientations.

It is helpful now to recall our definition of education. If education is understood not merely in a formal sense but also in a cultural sense, it is really a name for the total process by which a culture transmits and modifies its way of life. Education is inextricably involved in the present crisis—a fact epitomized by the conflict between those who see education mainly as transmission and those who see it mainly as modification and innovation.

A third term should be redefined, one that is necessary not only to this discussion but to those that follow: philosophy. In the preceding chapter it was rather narrowly regarded as the discipline concerned with the formulation of precise meaning; accordingly I have sought to be reasonably precise in my effort to give meaning to the terms crisis and education. I respect this use of philosophy very much, but it is not a sufficient definition. The expression of meaning is an important role that philosophy has played and should play. Nevertheless, it is only one role.

Another far more comprehensive definition is this: philosophy is the symbolic expression of culture. Every culture therefore has its own philosophy, although not necessarily formulated in sophisticated terminology or even written down. It is the effort of any organized group of people to express their way of life in some more or less consistent, unified way. Anthropologists often use a word for this: *ethos*. The ethos of a culture connotes its deepest meanings—meanings expressed in many forms through many symbolic media, not merely in words but in music, painting, dance, and other nonverbal media. This is the conception of philosophy that I would like you to consider here. We need to regard the conflicts besetting American educational philosophy as expressions of the ethos of our time, of an ethos in crisis.

Indeed, the philosophies of our age are themselves in crisis. Everywhere thoughtful people are searching for more adequate, honest expressions of the ethos of our time. So I would like you to keep the terms crisis, education, and philosophy in close interrelationship. All three are to be perceived in the context of culture, which is a name for the total environment that man himself has fashioned as he has lived with other men in the course of evolution.

Reactions to crisis: six patterns

Now, in such a setting, please consider this question: When traditional value orientations seem to be breaking down, what happens in a culture suffering from crisis to the efforts of men to understand and guide their respective ways of life?

Is it not obvious what happens? Men simply do not react in similar ways; rather, they react in radically different ways. At least six alternative patterns may be considered in which people respond to a time when the older guides to the good life no longer provide the directions and purposes which people everywhere, regardless of their particular cultures, seem to require.

The first of these ways may be called *skepticism*. A skeptic is simply a person who says: "There is no way out, really; we can't find a philosophy that is reliable, that can restore equilibrium." It is just not "in the cards." America is full of skeptics today, and not only philosophic skeptics. Some of this skepticism is indicated in the behavior of adolescents—in the fact that many young people have lost their sense of values, and are suffering from rootlessness, from a loss of faith in themselves and their world. This kind of phenomenon, which is occurring all over America today, is one expression of philosophic skepticism.

A second way that people react in times of crisis is to say, "We are all right. The only trouble is that we haven't taken full advantage of all the resources we have—intellectual, emotional, religious. We need to exploit a great variety of them, and when we do so we shall rediscover the vitality we need." The term that philosophers apply to this viewpoint—namely, that no one viewpoint will do but that it is desirable to mix many viewpoints together—is *eclecticism*.

Eclecticism, in brief, is the name for a philosophy consisting of parts of many philosophies. It denies that one can find the answers to the problems of life in any one outlook. Eclecticism has something to be said for it—certainly it is not dogmatic and it is open to many kinds of meaning. Yet it is not at all an adequate guide to the ethos needed in our age of crisis. It becomes a kind of intellectual opportunism in which one may follow one philosophy one day and another philosophy another day. This is illustrated in American politics when people shift from one candidate to another, from one kind of platform to another. It is illustrated in the arts and in other areas of culture. The eclectic may find comfort in not having to be very much committed to anything, but he is not a really unified individual. He possesses no ethos that can make sense of either his own life or the culture's life.

So, if neither skepticism nor eclecticism provides the philosophy we seek, what is left? What are the alternatives? Isn't it true that in times of confusion, some people always find the greatest security and comfort in that which is most customary and traditional to them? And so they try very hard to preserve and reinforce their heritage. They often contend that there is nothing seriously wrong with our culture if we would only restore the basic core of strength to be found in the great patterns of modern history. Strictly speaking, they are advocates of *conservatism* in that they wish, above all, to conserve the cultural heritage.

Another kind of reaction to crisis is to declare, "No, we can't just conserve. The conservative way has itself proved inadequate. We need to reach back much further into the past in order to discover the deepest roots of culture and thought." I call this the regressive way, but not in any derogatory sense. *Regressivism* simply favors a position toward life and the universe that prevailed at a much earlier time in the history of man.

Still another alternative, however, disagrees sharply with both conservatism and regressivism. Evolution, it argues, is never regressive, whether biological or cultural. To assume that we can find guidance in some nostalgic period of the remote past is no more legitimate than to devote ourselves mainly to conserving tradition. The answer to crisis, we are told, is to move forward gradually, to experiment cautiously, to try first this and then that modification in our habits, attitudes, and practices. You see immediately that this position advocates a kind of deliberative planning process, of gradual growth. Let us call it the viewpoint of *liberalism*.

Then there is a final alternative. Its proponents maintain that a great crisis requires equally great action and great purpose. Major crises of the past have never been overcome by any of the previous five ways. They are overcome only by rebuilding in new directions toward future goals and purposes that have not been achieved thus far. Such a view says, "We must reshape. We must renew the culture. Otherwise we are lost." In a precise sense, this is the viewpoint of *radicalism*.

So you see that there are at least six different ways in which people react philosophically (in one sense of the term) to crisis. All six have been manifested in America—the skeptical way, the eclectic way, the conservative way, the regressive way, the liberal way, and the radical way. Indeed, one symptom of the fact that American civilization is itself in a state of crisis is that no one of these choices is clearly dominant, yet that each of the six claims its own zealous advocates. Each appeals strongly to some, who are thus in conflict with others to whom different alternatives are more appealing.

Patterns in educational philosophy

You will note that we have been considering philosophy in terms of far-reaching cultural choices. Let us turn more explicitly now to educational philosophy. In America, one can discover skeptics in education, but even more eclectics. A few people believe in the Marxian philosophy of education. Others hold different beliefs. Nevertheless, by and large, the contention can be made that four major philosophies prevail in American educational theory today. These four represent more or less consistently the last four of the choices that I have epitomized.

To reconsider the choices in this new perspective, we may say that many people believe education should be primarily an agent for the conservation of culture. Others contend that education ought to regress to some great pattern of guidance from the classical past, for only such a pattern will give us what we require to restore cultural equilibrium. Still others believe that education can and should keep the culture moving forward slowly and experimentally; nothing is really wrong that cannot be corrected by this kind of learning and teaching. Finally, there are those who believe that education needs to become an agent, not merely of transmission or even of gradual modification, but of thoroughgoing changes in our culture.

The terms that are frequently applied to these major views are (1) *essentialism*, which is the educational philosophy concerned chiefly with the conservation of culture; (2) *perennialism*, which centers its attention in the kind of educational guidance provided by the classical thought of ancient Greece and medieval Europe; (3) *progressivism*, which is the philosophy of liberal, experimental education; and (4) *reconstructionism*, which believes that the contemporary crisis can be effectively attacked only by a radical educational policy and program of action.

Please remember that we are viewing these alternatives not as pure theories but as cultural interpretations of education. In my judgment, this is the only way that we can fully understand what they mean, what their roles are, and what they aim to achieve.

Essentialism can be further clarified if we approach its meaning adjectivally. The essentialists are most interested in what they consider to be most essential to education. Of course, the question at once arises, What is most essential? The answer for theorists of this persuasion is the tried and tested experiences, values, and institutions that have been conserved most firmly by tradition and have been proved by this very fact to be the best possible guide to educational practice.

It follows that the essentialist is one who ardently supports the study of traditional subject matters such as language and science, and traditional skills such as mathematics and grammar. At present, he is in a very influential position in America. Indeed, he has always been influential, but in recent years he has become still more so than in the earlier decades of this century. An explanation for this is to be found, not in the superiority of essentialist philosophers of education, although there are some excellent ones, but in the crisis which impels education to respond in one way or another. The essentialist responds by urging the conservation of customary ways of learning and living. This is a perfectly understandable emotional reaction to a time such as ours, just as it has been in other critical times. It helps greatly to explain the currently powerful influence of more conservative types of curriculum, as against, for example, the so-called "activity programs" that were previously characteristic of some modern American schools.

Next, let me say a little about perennialism as educational theory. Here again we are helped by an adjective, in this case perennial. Please remember what the term means in botany: a perennial flower is one that grows season after season without new seeding. It is a constant, "everlasting" flower.

What the perennialist in education seeks are the "flowers" or principles of truth, beauty, and goodness which renew themselves each season and each epoch without replanting. He thinks that the seedbed of these principles is ancient Greek civilization—especially the philosophy of Plato and Aristotle, who thought that they had discovered the everlasting, permanent principles of reality that in turn could provide the eternal guides of man's destiny. The perennialist in education believes that the whole program of education should be geared to a search for these principles and on elucidation of them. These principles then become the guideposts by which cultural equilibrium may be restored.

The third philosophy, progressivism, is pinpointed by the adjective progressive. What do we ordinarily mean when we say that a person is progressive? Well, at least we mean a person who believes in progress—in the gradual bettering of man's lot. But this does not mean that progress is automatic. No one can be assured that life will get better and better. At best, says the progressivist, progress is always possible.

Nevertheless, progress can be achieved if we want it enough. We can make life richer and finer than it is now. But we can make it so only as we human beings mobilize ourselves to utilize our intelligence, in order to solve problems in the way scientists do. In other words, we can try out experimentally new ways of dealing with old difficulties, and gradually move forward as we succeed with these new ways. This, at heart, is what I understand progressivism to be as a philosophy of education. When you hear of that much criticized program, progressive education, remember that the term stands for a method of education which enables people to progress by learning how to experiment in dealing with the genuine problems of their own lives.

Thus the school should become a center in which experimentation constantly takes place, a center in which children learn from the very first years how to think and act scientifically—and not merely in the field of physics or biology, but above all in all sorts of human relations.

The trouble is that most people simply do not know how to think or act experimentally in solving human problems. They fall back upon superstition, upon dogma, upon pre-established authority, upon all kinds of dubious solutions, rather than upon the only way that assures genuine progress. This is the way of testing ideas carefully, slowly, in the laboratory of culture.

And now, reconstructionism. This viewpoint, again, may be best understood if we take the key word apart. What does it mean to *reconstruct* something? Does it not often mean to take the materials, the resources, and the experiences that are available from the past and the present, and to undertake a thorough job of redesigning strongly, audaciously, and often beautifully, for the future?

The reconstructionist, then, goes along part way with the progressivist. But he is even more emphatic in insisting that education is, or at least should be, primarily an agent for rebuilding the culture. He is radical in the strict sense, for example, that he believes this rebuilding should be prepared to break many precedents. In an age of crisis such as ours, precedents often hold back change and thereby delay the alterations in cultural arrangements that are required.

Now you perceive that there are really two pairs of philosophies of education: on the one side, the essentialist-perennialist pair; on the other side, the progressivist-reconstructionist pair. Please imagine these as a kind of continuum of culture—culture in this sense coming into being through the ability of man to learn and to teach what he acquires from generation to generation. Philosophies of education, no matter how sophisticated their formulations, appear in this context as theoretical ways of providing rationales by which cultures survive and evolve. Essentialism and perennialism belong primarily on the transmitting side of the continuum, progressivism and reconstructionism on the innovating side.

← — Reconstructionism — → — ← — Progressivism — → — ← — Essentialism — → — ← — Perennialism — →

Perennialism, moreover, becomes a philosophy of education toward the right end of the cultural continuum and reconstructionism toward the left end. Perennialism, though it does not ignore the future, wishes not only to preserve the past but to regress to classical patterns for its major guidance. Reconstructionism, though it needs the past, presses us forward toward the future. And between perennialism and reconstructionism, progressivism is also at the left but not as far; it is nearer the center. Essentialism is toward the right but not as far as perennialism; it is also nearer the center. So the continuum leads from left to right, with reconstructionism in political terms the most radical, progressivism the most liberal, essentialism the most conservative, and perennialism the most regressive.

Please note the term continuum. I want to convey through the broken lines of the diagram that the four philosophies are not sharply separable. They are not to be regarded as distinct categories which have no relation with each other. A continuum suggests that each flows into the other, and that there is some relation among all. Actually, certain features of essentialism and perennialism are to be found in progressivism and reconstructionism, and vice versa. This does not make them eclectic. Each of these philosophies borrows something from the others, but each fuses what is borrowed into its own organic, unified position.

We may clarify this point by noting a paradox. In a sense, perennialism and reconstructionism are at opposite ends of the continuum; yet it is a good principle of dialectics that opposite ideas or experiences often have more in common than those that are only partly different. This is true of perennialism and reconstructionism in one respect: both philosophies recognize the need for goals, the need for strong purposes. Both are dissatisfied with essentialism and progressivism partly, if not primarily, because these do not provide such goals. Both are "goal-centered" philosophies. Both contend that the crisis of our time is characterized to a considerable degree by the bankruptcy of traditional purposes and by the necessity of purposes that have not been successfully formulated in terms appropriate to this crisis.

But the nature of the goals which the two philosophies urge is extremely different. The perennialist finds his goals in eternal reality itself; they are already there, waiting for achievement; they are written into the very structure of nature and of man. The reconstructionist disagrees with this kind of absolutism and insists that the goals needed for our time have to be built out of man's experience. There is nothing eternal or inherent about them, nor does nature guarantee their achievement. If they are to be achieved at all, they will be achieved because people agree upon them sufficiently to act so that they may be realized. The reconstructionist here allies with the progressivist again in denying any predetermined direction within the course of reality. All such interrelations make clear that it would be a gross distortion to regard any one of the four philosophies of education as contained in a kind of intellectual box walled off from the other three.

In this chapter I have not pretended to deal in any detailed way with the meaning of major philosophies of education. My purpose has been to present a sketch of the directions in which they are moving in America, and above all to consider these directions in the setting of contemporary dislocations and in the context of education conceived of as an agent of both cultural transmission and modification.

The remaining chapters will frequently refer to these philosophies. Before we are through, their significance should be somewhat clearer than at present. It is necessary, however, to make one remaining point entirely clear now. I am myself identified with the reconstructionist philosophy of education. I am proudly identified with it. Thus everything I have said and everything I shall say is conditioned directly or indirectly by this point of view. I say this now, not to ask you to accept my position, but rather to put you on your guard against it. Every teacher has an obligation to indicate where he stands in his own beliefs, in his own values, in his own choices, so that students will know that he is not impartial (and what teacher is ever completely impartial?). In this spirit, I invite you to be critical toward me and to decide for yourself whether or not you can accept part or all of the reconstructionist position, or of any alternative. I have deep respect for each of the philosophies that I have defined. Moreover, it is important to note that, in America, the reconstructionist is the least popular, perhaps the least known, of those we have considered. So if you want to join hands with the majority of American philosophers of education, do not become a reconstructionist.

4/ *Toward a Reconstructed Philosophy of Education*

What I have been trying to say so far may be reduced to one proposition: the problems of education can only be understood in the context of the problems of culture. Too often, we as educators look at ourselves in a narrow and artificial framework. The problems of education should be taken out of their professional, academic setting and put where they really belong—in the mainstream of the period of civilization through which we are passing.

Chapter 3 presented an outline of conflicting theories of education in America today. These four philosophies of education may be called (1) the essentialist, (2) the progressivist, (3) the perennialist, and (4) the reconstructionist. Although this listing is by no means comprehensive, these at least may be discussed. They should be approached not as philosophies of education, merely, but as alternative ways through which education in America attempts to bring itself into vital relationship with cultural transmission and cultural modification—the bipolar orientation of education in every culture. The four viewpoints are here regarded, then, as symbolic expressions by American philosophers of the role that education plays or should play in serving our period of civilization.

It should be reiterated also that these viewpoints overlap. Especially, they may be treated as two pairs of philosophies. One pair may be considered as the essentialist-perennialist continuum. Although they are different in many ways, essentialism and perennialism are similar in that they are concerned more with the function of education as cultural transmission, reenforcement, or conservation, than with any of its other functions.

The other pair of philosophies is on a continuum also—the progressivist-reconstructionist continuum. Education is conceived by them primarily as an agent of cultural change, modification, or rebuilding. If the two pairs of philosophies are set side by side, the first two appear to offer a rationale for education as a way of maintaining traditional patterns of living, thinking, and acting. The other pair regard education primarily as a way of helping to direct the culture toward new cultural arrangements.

From this point on, I shall be talking very largely from the point of view of the reconstructionist philosophy of education. First we shall consider some general characteristics of reconstructionism, and then three or four more specific features.

Some characteristics of reconstructionism

The first general characteristic has been treated in the preceding lectures, but I must note it once more. I do not hesitate to call reconstructionism a "crisis philosophy." It is a crisis philosophy in terms not only of education but of culture. For, if we remember that education is part and parcel of culture—indeed, a creation of culture—it follows that a crisis philosophy of education must presuppose a crisis philosophy of culture. Let us recall some of the things said earlier about the nature of the crisis of our time. For example, we are living in an age that is capable, on the one hand, of destroying mankind overnight, and on the other hand, of producing a higher level of civilization on a world scale than man has ever known. We are truly at a crossroad. But many of us are not at all sure which of the two forks we are going to follow—the one toward destruction or the one toward reconstruction.

The reconstructionist is, of course, very clear as to which road mankind should take, but he is not at all clear as to which road it will take. He has no assurance whatsoever that we are wise enough to choose the road toward reconstruction rather than that toward destruction. But he is convinced that the choice is clear, and that the least education can do is to devote its utmost energy, its utmost responsibility, to making certain that the peoples of the world choose the road of reconstruction.

Another general feature of this philosophy follows closely and may deepen the previous contention made about the nature of crisis itself. Let us reemphasize the important part that values play in the analysis and interpretation of crisis. For the truth is, of course, that every crisis centers in a dislocation of the value patterns by which all cultures are guided. In such a time many members of the culture simply do not know what to believe as to what is good, as to what is desirable, as to what is purposeful. So many conflicting choices confront them that often they are not sure which choice to make. The reconstructionist contends, therefore, that much of mankind suffers today not only from institutional disequilibrium but from moral confusion and uncertainty. But he maintains also that there are fresh and powerful values to be discovered and to become committed to. The search for and delineation of these values is one of the highest priorities of education.

Reconstructionism is above all, then, a philosophy of values, a philosophy of ends, a philosophy of purposes. It believes that you and I, as teachers and citizens, have the obligation to analyze critically what is wrong with the values that we have been holding and then to decide about the values that we should be holding. The remainder of these lectures will discuss at considerable length the question of the values, the purposes, the moral commitments for which men everywhere should be searching if we are to resolve the dangerous confusions and conflicts which plague us and threaten us with destruction.

One further general characteristic is that reconstructionism, no less than any philosophy worthy of the name, is by no means wholly new. If we define philosophy as the attempt of any culture to give meaning to itself, and so to its ethos, then reconstructionism must in many ways be built upon the rich thinking and experience of other philosophies of life and education. Reconstructionism borrows much from other philosophies, and makes no pretense to the contrary.

From essentialism, for example, it borrows the principle that all education is inevitably transmissive. One of the fundamental tasks of teaching-learning is certainly that of maintaining the continuity of cultural experience.

From progressivism, the reconstructionist borrows particularly the key principle that processes of cultural change are possible through intelligent action. I know of no man in the history of philosophy who has done as much to help us understand the meaning of intelligent action as the greatest philosopher of education in the history of America, John Dewey. In his view, intelligent action should be integral with the processes of education, and both of these in turn should become inseparable from the processes of cultural change.

From the perennialist, I would choose as an important example of influence his insistence that life must be purposeful, that life must have clear goals. To be sure, the perennialist's goals are usually dissimilar to those of the reconstructionist. But the common recognition that the good life must be goal centered and purposeful is one which brings both philosophies together and causes both of them to pay tribute to the influence of such geniuses as Plato and Aristotle.

Some requirements of reconstructionism

So much for some general characteristics of reconstructionism. Let us now try to be more specific. First of all, since the reconstructionist, being a crisis philosopher, places heavy stress upon clear, unequivocal goals and purposes, the primary task of education is that of formulating, implementing, and validating such purposes. This contention is tied up with what was said above about the importance of values, for all purposes are saturated with values.

The reconstructionist, accordingly, is searching for what we earlier called, in common with some American social scientists, a value orientation. Is it possible to develop a value orientation that is sufficiently defensible and unified to give us the purposes we now need—one that can galvanize and channel our activities?

Where are such purposes to be found? They will not, I think, be found merely through philosophic analysis. They will be found, if at all, through understanding the abnormal nature of our time, and through recognition of what is required by such a time.

Now there is one requirement today which overshadows all others—a requirement which I noted in my opening chapter and to which I shall return in my closing one. This is a world civilization so powerful, so unified, and so committed to the values we shall presently describe that it can successfully combat and destroy the forces which could lead to the destruction of mankind. World civilization is the great magnetic purpose which education requires today. What does this purpose mean?

Vast problems at once arise when one seriously considers such an encompassing purpose. Certainly it becomes a primary task of education to attack the gigantic difficulties in the way of achieving world civilization. For, as these difficulties are analyzed, the meaning of world civilization itself becomes more and more clear.

Despite the hazards of generalizing about reconstructionism, one thing can be said now that will indicate how it is different, in substantial degree at least, from other philosophies on our continuum: the purpose of a world civilization is a radical purpose. It is radical in that it is a thoroughgoing and future-directed goal for mankind. Thus far in its history, mankind has never achieved a world civilization—not even remotely. The world has been split into warring camps that expend much of their energy and resources in hating each other and trying to destroy each other. Hate and destruction are disvalues that often seem to have been more conspicuous in the life of man than the values of love and cooperation and construction. Hence, to propose such a goal as world civilization in which peoples of all races, all nations, all colors, and all creeds join together in the common purpose of a peaceful world, united under the banner of international order, is truly a radical purpose. I suggest to my fellow teachers that should they devote themselves to this great purpose, and in turn help young people to assume responsibility for its achievement, they will become radical teachers. And this, says the reconstructionist, is precisely what they should become.

One more point about the meaning of this supreme purpose may be made in a preliminary way. It is obvious that many people in the world are already prepared to agree on the purpose of world civilization. Where they disagree is on the nature of the world civilization that they favor. To the communist, for instance, the idea of world civilization is perfectly congenial, provided that the civilization is built on communist principles. The remarkable Pope John XXIII also wanted a world civilization. But of course he wanted it in terms of the perennialist conception of man and the universe.

So it is necessary to go further. We need to inquire into the precise meanings of different conceptions of the central purpose. Education should carefully consider, for example, what the communist is advocating. Any school system which prevents children from studying communism fairly, objectively, and thoroughly is not a responsible school system. The same is true in the study of, let us say, the proposals of the Roman Catholic Church; we need to understand critically and comparatively what it advocates also. Similarly we should understand as fully as we can the purpose of world civilization which reconstructionists, or people close to them in viewpoint, most strongly favor.

The essence of this purpose centers in the conception of democracy. We should carefully examine what democracy means. It is, of course, the hope of reconstructionists that if enough people understand what democracy really means, rather than resorting to superficial labels that sound pleasant but mean little, they will come to agree that the kind of world civilization they want most is a democratic world civilization. Here again, we are brought back to the question of value orientations, because democracy itself points toward a definite value orientation.

Reconstructionism and democracy

What, then, is the nature of a democratic value orientation? At least this: it is one in which man believes in himself, in his capacity to direct himself and to govern himself in relation to his fellows. Politically, this means that a world civilization of the kind reconstructionists advocate is one in which fundamental policies are determined by the majority of people of the world, and in which, at the same time, minorities have the right to criticize and to dissent from policies established by the majority. This does not mean dissent in the sense of disregarding or disobeying such policies, but in the sense of having the privilege of criticizing them and attempting freely to persuade the majority that they are wrong.

Democracy as a political philosophy, therefore, is also bi-polar. It cannot possibly function unless both of these principles are constantly at work: majority policy making and minority criticism. Each is necessary to the other. The value orientation behind this bipolarity is a deep conviction that human beings, ordinary human beings in the long run, have more common sense and good judgment with regard to what is ultimately good for them than any one else does—any leader or group of leaders, no matter how allegedly benevolent or wise they may claim to be. Unless we earnestly believe this, and unless we as teachers have profound confidence in the capacity of the majority of people to make the best basic decisions regarding policy, we do not accept democracy.

By this kind of test, I am afraid that we could discover quite a few teachers and students in America who really do not accept democracy, even though they are quick to pay lip service to it. Test yourself: if you want to see the principle of political bipolarity extended to world civilization, you believe that you, in concert with your fellows all over the world, are the final, ultimate judges of what is best for you. You are the ones to establish policy—no minority, no superauthority, no special-interest group—only you. Thus you must have faith not only in yourself but in your fellow citizens. If you possess this faith, you believe in democracy; if you do not possess it, you do not believe in democracy regardless of the words you use.

Means and resources in reconstructionism

We have focused thus far upon ends and purposes. But reconstructionism is not just a philosophy of ends—indeed, all philosophies of education worthy of the name are also concerned with means. For education, as an agency through which cultures transmit and modify themselves, is inevitably a process, too. Consequently, we must ask: What is the reconstructionist view of education as means?

For one thing, education as means is only strong when education as an end is strong. We need to know what we want, where we want to go, what our objectives are. Then we can begin to work out ways by which to achieve them. Here is one of the points at which the reconstructionist modifies the progressivist philosophy. The latter emphasizes that ends emerge out of the means we use: if we develop effective means, the ends will eventually come into view. The reconstructionist philosophy emphasizes more strongly that means are also shaped by the ends we decide upon and commit ourselves to. That is, if we are clear about where we are going, we will be more likely to develop the necessary processes by which to get there. To be sure, ends and means are necessary to each other. Nevertheless, education should now concern itself much more deeply and directly than hitherto with the great ends of civilization.

Another definite characteristic of the reconstructionist approach to means, one which could make some claim to distinctiveness, is its stronger-than-average insistence upon the limitations in man's rationality. In many ways, man possesses tremendously powerful unrational drives, both within himself and in his relations with other men. If we are to channel the forces of education effectively toward achievement of such a great purpose as democratic world civilization, it is necessary for us to recognize and utilize these powerful unrational forces—the forces of emotion, the forces of hostility and conflict, as well as the forces of love and harmony. Reconstructionism searches for fresh insights into the nature of man, individually and collectively, in order to understand how he may capitalize upon his energies to the utmost in behalf of imperative new goals.

Where may we search for these resources? Two in particular stand out as intellectual mountain peaks of the last hundred years. The first is the young science of psychiatry. Here, of course, one immediately thinks of that giant in the study of man's emotional complexities, Sigmund Freud (although others as diverse as Carl Jung and Harry Stack Sullivan may also occur to you). More firmly than the other major philosophies of education, reconstructionism contends that sophisticated awareness of these complexities is now so necessary that no teacher can be competently prepared for his work unless he is acquainted with the main principles and practices of this rapidly growing science.

The second major resource for understanding the unrational dimension of man's nature is to be found in those social sciences which examine the phenomena of group behavior, especially class behavior. Here the greatest of all pioneers is, I think, Karl Marx, a profound student of society who exposed the unrational behavior of people, not as individuals, but in their organized social and economic relations. The modern teacher needs to become familiar with the chief contributions of Marx and of later scholars who have modified his interpretation.

Thus the reconstructionist philosophy of education insists upon analysis of the unrational factors in life, both from the point of view of the individual and from the point of view of the group. This is not to say that education as means wishes merely to encourage the release of these unrational factors. This is to say that education as an agency of cultural rebuilding cannot effectively operate rationally unless it takes into full consideration the strength of the unrational. There is a paradox here. It is sometimes contended that the Marxist has no respect for rationality because he stresses the conflicting and sometimes violent nature of the struggle between classes. But this contention overlooks a deeper assumption in Marxian theory: men can never become rational as long as they conceal from themselves their own unrational social behavior. Freudians maintain the same paradox with regard to the individual.

Socrates said twenty-five hundred years ago, "Know thyself." Marx might have said, "If thou art to know thyself, become conscious of thy class relationships." Freud might have said, "To know thyself, examine thy inner emotional forces." The reconstructionist wishes to transform education into a powerful means for social change toward world civilization. But to accomplish this we must learn how to estimate and direct our energies on all levels of personal and cultural nature. The means are ultimately rational, to be sure, but only if and when they succeed in recognizing the power of the unrational.

Let me try to put together what I have been saying. Both the progressivist and the reconstructionist strongly believe in education as cultural modification. They urge you and me as teachers, and as potential if not actual leaders in education, to regard our institution as an agency of change as well as an agency of stabilization.

I am convinced that it makes a world of difference to us whether we approach our work believing primarily that education is a power for the renewal of civilization, or whether we enter with the dominant attitude that our main task is to transmit and to preserve the social heritage. A persuasive case can be made for either approach, and, of course, no teacher can or should hold either one to the complete exclusion of the other. But the reconstructionist view is that, in a crisis age such as our own, the former of the two approaches is much to be preferred to the latter.

Supposing that you agree, many questions remain. How, for example, can the reconstructionist theory be made to work in practice?

What is the significance of its very large and difficult ideas for us as everyday teachers, confronted as we are with a host of daily tasks, routine assignments, chronic frustrations, limited resources? These are urgent questions, and I hope we may partially deal with them as we proceed.

But let me say now that the reconstructionist point of view means fundamental alteration in the curriculum of the schools all the way from kindergarten up through the high schools, the colleges, and adult education. The processes of learning and teaching will also be radically altered. Finally, the control of education, including its administration and policy-making, will have to be changed. Thus, the curriculum, the teaching-learning process, and the control of education will all undergo transformation. This, again, is what is implied by a democratically radical philosophy. A philosophy which endorses minor, patchwork changes cannot achieve the required goals. Only a far-reaching, reconstructive approach to education as both ends and means will serve an age such as ours.

Frontiers in Educational Theory

The theme which now comes into sharper focus is the need for a philosophy of education that can effectively cope with our crisis culture. The most widely influential philosophies of education, in America at least, all recognize in varying degrees that the present period of history is a hazardous one, but none of them offers a theory or a program sufficient to deal with the crisis. They are not sufficient for various reasons. Perhaps the most fundamental, however, are that they neither analyze the nature of the world situation searchingly enough, nor do they propose the kinds of reform and action that such analysis impels.

Since I state that the more traditional and more popular theories of education in America are found to be inadequate, let me hasten to add that the theory of reconstructionism is also inadequate. It is far from a completed theory. It is very much on the "cutting edge" of thought and experimentation. It inevitably confronts problems that are often baffling. Much of the research that is most relevant to its tasks is only beginning. It needs to come to grips with developments in philosophic, social, and educational theory which are often uncrystallized and still immature. Please, then, try to regard reconstructionism, not as a doctrine, not as a finished theory, but as a challenge to you and me to confront many puzzling questions. I invite my fellow teachers to join with me in the search for answers. Above all, I invite them to help in building not only an effective theory but an effective program of education as power.

Let us consider six, among many more, intriguing problem areas to illustrate the kinds of tasks that you and I are required to undertake. Let us label these problem areas as follows: (1) logical analysis; (2) sociological realism; (3) existentialism; (4) creativity; (5) social-self-realization; and (6) evolution. In turning now to some preliminary characterizations, I contend that each one of the six has vast importance not only for reconstructionist theory but for our practical, daily classroom work. If this importance is not always immediately evident, we must not be impatient. The connections between theory and practice are often elusive and complex.

Logical analysis

Turning to the first frontier, logical analysis, I need perhaps only reiterate what has been said about the need of precisely defining our terms, such as education itself, or crisis, or philosophy. Logical analysis, a popular movement not only in American philosophy today but also in European philosophy, is concerned with refining and clarifying meanings, with analyzing language so that we actually say what we mean to say. Numerous philosophers today contend that this is all that philosophy can do—a contention now shared by several of the ablest young philosophers of education in America. The only real task of philosophy in our profession, they say, is to help you and me, as teachers or administrators, to learn how to express ourselves accurately and therefore meaningfully.

We educators can learn much from logical analysis. We are notoriously careless about our language. We toss about all kinds of vague, loose words and phrases which no one really understands. Indeed, can you think of any profession as guilty of this kind of symbolic carelessness? Logical analysis provides a kind of intellectual cautery. It forces us to discipline our efforts at communication. Teachers who study logical analysis are going to ask much oftener than they do now, "What do you mean? What do you mean?"

I have heard one distinguished interpreter of American education and culture assert that over half the time in the average American classroom is lost, simply because neither students nor teachers are really hearing one another. There is a lot of noise, of course—almost everybody makes believe that he is understanding. But the truth is, if this authority is right, that for a shockingly large part of the average school day almost no one is understanding. Logical analysis does, I think, make a contribution from which not only reconstructionists can benefit, but all of us.

Sociological realism

The second frontier, sociological realism, performs two important roles in building the needed new philosophy of education. The first role is to correct defects in the first frontier: logical analysis does not begin to consider sufficiently the social influences that operate upon the words we use, the meanings we share. Logical analysis, in other words, is almost too logical. It much too simply solves the problem of meanings by isolating them from their human context.

The sociological realist argues that many symbols can never be understood merely by precise analysis, because they are also heavily influenced by the reality of the cultural world around us—a reality which shapes our reactions and our judgments, although we are often quite unconscious of its influence. Sociological realism, in other words, helps us to realize how often what we consider to be an experience of the truth or the good is conditioned by the social, the economic, or the political perspective from which we look upon that experience.

Here Marx's influence is at work, of course. As I implied earlier, what Marx taught, and what many scholars have elaborated and qualified since, is that men are divided into classes, and that their outlook on life is frequently and deeply shaped by the class to which they are most closely attached. People who belong to the upper classes, for example, usually look at their culture through different pairs of spectacles than do people who belong to the lower classes. So-called impartial truth about human experience does not occur anywhere nearly as often as truth which is colored and formed by one's class orientation. The sociological realist helps us to correct our distortions by making us more conscious of the fact that we all have them.

Important educational implications may be readily derived from sociological realism. One is the evidence of research studies that teachers in America, for example, are overwhelmingly middle class in the way they evaluate themselves and their students. Thus they tend to judge the attitudes and conduct of children by their own values, even though many children come from other levels of the culture than their own. Theirs are usually middle-class spectacles, and the defect in their vision cannot be corrected merely by logical analysis, no matter how skillfully it may be applied in educational practice.

Another role of sociological realism is perhaps only a different way of stating the point that I have just been making. Sociological realism helps us to realize more clearly than otherwise that we human beings are never wholly impartial toward the values of life; each of us almost invariably prefers values of one kind rather than another, and we try to accept them and live by them even when they prove to be in conflict or confused or inconsistent. To recall a previous term, we require some kind of value orientation. Hence, sociological realism leads us to the forthright admission that teachers, too, are not and cannot be impartial. Like other human beings, we have our own value orientations.

In an age of crisis, however, a serious problem arises from conflict among alternatives. What choice are we going to make? To what value orientation are we prepared to give our first allegiance? In choosing to be partial to one set of values as against another, you and I are compelled to be realistic about the world we live in and desire to live in. But this kind of realism demands sociological awareness of our class position and of the values of which this position approves or disapproves. If you agree with the reconstructionist, the value orientation you accept may no longer be in harmony with the middle-class outlook as typically expressed. It will have to be on the side of the forces who are fighting for a democratic world civilization and against those forces who are fighting against it. These forces are by no means primarily the middle classes; they are chiefly the working and farming peoples who still constitute, certainly outside of America, a large proportion of the earth's population.

The choice is not easy, and teachers cannot afford to treat it lightly. I wish you to remember, however, that you are already partial to some pattern of values, and to ask yourselves whether this is the choice you most deeply prefer. Try to be as conscious as you can about the choice you make, even though this may demand a good deal of courage. Remember that some kind of choice, whether easy or difficult, is unavoidable. But know what you are doing.

Existentialism

The third of our problem areas is existentialism. In America existentialism is probably, next to logical analysis, the most popular recent development in philosophy. And just as one finds a group of able young men and women who are beginning to make contributions to American educational theory in terms of logical analysis, so several others are beginning to make interesting contributions by way of existentialism.

I call your attention to the fact that both of these developments, and indeed sociological realism as well, are much more European in their origin and expression than they are American. The fountainhead of logical analysis is Austria. Sociological realism comes originally from Germany. Existentialism emerged in Denmark, and flowered in Germany and France. This bit of history is interesting because it indicates that at the present time American philosophy is not as distinctive or creative as it was half a century or more ago when pragmatism was the great philosophic rising star. There are no John Deweys or William Jameses on the intellectual scene today. Rather, to a great extent, we seem to be going through a period of amendment to European thought.

Reconstructionism also readily concedes its indebtedness to Europe. Yet it seeks to become a philosophy of education which is neither merely American nor merely European, but cosmopolitan in world outlook. Existentialism, though European in derivation, reflects something of this universal quality.

What then is existentialism? And why is it important to the rebuilding of a philosophy of education? Unfortunately, one discovers relatively little common ground upon which all the great existentialists stand.

One way to approach it, however, is through our second frontier idea, sociological realism. Both this and existentialism agree on at least one proposition. This is that existence precedes rational formulations or systematizations of existence. The sociological realist argues that class interests and class conflicts precede and influence rational judgments about them. The existentialist holds that behind and beneath human existence is a fundamental, unrational, primordial self upon which is gradually built a more or less rational, logical understanding and interpretation. The existentialist, in briefest terms, is trying to tell us that each one of us is imprisoned in his own being, and that philosophy is only able at best to offer a kind of supplementary explanation of the fact of his own being. The sciences of man therefore follow, they do not precede, this ultimate fact of the self's existence.

But there is another side of existentialism—that of the non-self, of the being of the universe itself. Here, too, we are told that an overwhelming, infinite reality exists both before and after speculative interpretations of that reality. The existentialist is really trying, as I understand him, to deepen the meaning of being, the meaning of both subjective and objective reality. The being of the self is ultimately inseparable from the being of the universe.

Existentialism is also trying to help us face the truth that there is something dreadful about reality. This dreadfulness centers in the mystery and inevitability of death. The great religions of the world have all tried in one way or another to account for death, thereby proving how important it is to the meaning of human existence. But most existentialists tell us that the great religious answers are simply wishful, pathetic hopes that the mystery and dread of death may be assuaged. Death is emptiness, nothingness, nonbeing. This fact of nonbeing, this fact of death, produces in most human beings a deep sense of anxiety—anxiety over the unknown, over the infinite spacelessness and timelessness of afterlife.

Thus the existentialist refuses to accept standard theological answers to the perplexity of death. Rather, he asks us to recognize the inescapability of one's own being and of the being of the universe, to realize the nonbeing of death, but to live courageously in spite of this realization. This, at least, is the kind of meaning that existentialism through its leading American interpreter, Paul Tillich, has been conveying to me.

Creativity

Creativity is our fourth frontier. It is interesting that a number of discerning scholars have begun to recognize the relevance of existentialism for creativity. For what the latter idea means, first of all, is that the human being, or sometimes a whole group of human beings (as in an orchestra or dance or drama), expresses his or its own unique significance as originally, imaginatively, and honestly as possible. This, I think, is what the existentialist is trying to convey to the artist. He is urging him to "state himself" in the most authentic way he can—to do so even though that statement may drive him to the deepest depths of personal agony.

I have come to appreciate better the great Dutch impressionist artist, Vincent van Gogh, since my acquaintance with existentialism. He was a genuine artist of self and universe; his paintings radiate the integrity of his own existence, and millions of spectators respond to them with a sense of identification far more eloquent than words. They have shared, through the miracle of pigment, van Gogh's highly personal celebration of the wonder and the terror of existence.

Another characteristic of creativity is that it is always apparently characterized by a moment of discovery, a moment that occurs like a flash of lightning after long periods of slow, only partly self-conscious incubation. This mysterious event, often called insight, is crucial to the creative act. I say "mysterious" because, after much research, we still fail to understand fully what the act means. Here it is well to recall the preceding discussion of the unrational, as developed by the psychoanalytic sciences. Freud and other psychoanalysts assist us in understanding this mechanism of discovery, of creative insight, whether expressed in a poem or a musical phrase or an architectural design. To grasp its import, we are compelled to explore the caverns of the unconscious, and to realize how much of the human psyche resides in that darkly fascinating sphere.

Social-self-realization

The fifth frontier idea has been termed social-self-realization—a term that I have found useful as a kind of shorthand symbol for the value orientation which I advocate, and which I believe can be defended because it resolves the chief confusions and conflicts that must arise in an age of crisis over choices among values. Since I shall have more to say about this, let me here simply define social-self-realization as the supreme, encompassing value of human life. As a goal, it requires that the purpose to which each human being should dedicate himself is to fulfill his maximum potentialities and powers both individually and in cooperative relationship with others—that is to say, socially.

The theory of social-self-realization is not in many ways new. But it is new at least in one important respect: to a greater degree than any value theory of history, it is grounded in a scientific understanding of man. Indeed, one may contend that for the first time in his long struggle to understand himself, man now finds it possible to establish a value orientation that can begin to be validated in terms of scientific knowledge. This value orientation is summarized by the term social-self-realization.

Let me restate the definition. Social-self-realization as a value symbolizes the highest human purpose. It is the realization of the capacity of the self to measure up to its fullest, most satisfying powers in cooperative relationship with other selves. One of the most important ways, moreover, in which we reach social-self-realization is through creativity. No person and no group of persons can achieve social-self-realization without at the same time being authentically, originally expressive. Social-self-realization is the ethical manifestation of the esthetic meaning of creativity.

Evolution

Evolution, the sixth and last frontier idea chosen for discussion, is not as recent in formulation as some of the others in our group. You know, of course, that Charles Darwin's *Origin of Species* was published in 1859, and that today, over one hundred years later, it is still recognized as one of the supreme contributions to science. Yet most of us have hardly begun to recognize the vast importance of evolution for the theory and practice of education. This was made plain again when scholars all over the world reexamined Darwin's ideas in order to celebrate the centennial of his great work.

Evolution speaks to us in scientific terms as social-self-realization speaks to us in ethical terms. Man is capable of becoming his own master because man is the one animal on earth able to guide his own evolution. All other animals (with the partial exception of those scientifically bred) are effects of the accidental concomitance of genetic variations, and they have nothing to say about the next step in their own evolution. But man, because he is self-conscious, because he is creative, because he is able to respect and control his own powers, can say to himself: "I am going to direct the course of my evolution toward whatever purposes I and my fellowmen decide upon."

This is also what the reconstructionist is trying to say in a variety of ways. Let us transform education into a gigantic agency through which man shapes his own evolution toward social-self-realization, toward maximum creativity. But if he is to do so, man must know where he wants to go, what his supreme purposes are. He possesses the power, but thus far he does not know how to release this power, or for what ends. Yet, among all animals, he alone can decide what he wants. I suggest that the moment has come for this decision. The first obligation of mankind in an age of crisis is to direct the evolutionary process toward the goal of a world democratic civilization. Here is the goal of evolution on our planet. We can achieve it, if we wish. Whether we shall or not is the most urgent question of our time.

The six concepts sketched above—logical analysis, sociological realism, existentialism, creativity, social-self-realization, and evolution—were earlier described as "problem areas." This was intentional: each frontier idea is fraught with disturbing questions, with intriguing fields for fresh research, and with challenges to educational theory and practice. Reconstructionism has by no means assimilated their rich implications or traced the intricate relationships among all of them. It does, however, regard them as illustrative of provocative new opportunities for the remaking of education throughout the world.

6/

Frontiers in Educational Practice

A colleague of mine used to remark that the most practical thing a teacher can accomplish in preparing for his profession is to become theoretical. What he meant by this paradox was that no one can be a good practitioner of education, a really good one, unless he possesses a consistent theory upon which his practice rests. From this point of view, it may be said that most teachers in training do not acquire nearly enough theory. They have all been told how to do things in so-called "methods" courses, but they have not acquired the ability to deal with the fundamental issues and principles which alone provide techniques with meaning and vitality.

But now, having argued for theory, I must violate my own mandate by turning to aspects of practice. Let us consider how the six frontiers of educational theory already outlined may be applied to a few concrete educational problems. All of these frontiers are infinitely fruitful for educational practice, and many of their implications have not yet been explored. I hope that you will explore them much further than I am able to do here.

Logical analysis

Let us go back to the first frontier, logical analysis, which centers in the contention that philosophy is a discipline enabling us to validate the symbols we use—to determine precisely the meaning of what we are saying. I underscore the point made earlier that logical analysis provides an important challenge to us in education. We ought to worry much more than we do about the frequent ambiguity of the words we toss around in our classrooms and in education courses. Through logical analysis, we can make sure that communication between students and teachers is more reliable, more precise. Here, surely, is one contribution to educational practice of far-reaching import.

But how does one reach such precision of meaning? Although I have insisted that logical analysis does not have the whole answer to this question, it does focus upon one very crucial requirement. All concepts must be referred to experience. Evidence must be derived from the observable phenomena or data of nature against which concepts can be checked.

The logical analyst severely criticizes much of the language we use largely because it has no such reference to experience. On the contrary, language is often little more than a vacuum of abstractions. He contends that the history of philosophy, for example, is loaded with words that are meaningless, because they have no connection with anything that we can test—with anything that we can check factually, empirically. Much of speculative philosophy has been verbal nonsense.

What is the practical implication of this argument? Is it not that you and I as teachers should become as conscious as we can of the necessity to bring the symbols we use back to experience—back to the facts, back to the actual environments of learners? This is an important lesson that I am sure most of us in education have not learned at all well. The logical analyst can help us to learn it much better.

One more point about the first of the frontier ideas in terms of its practical implications. What the logical analyst is saying is, in a way, nothing new at all: the most reliable guide to the truth about man and about nature is the method of science. This method alone enables us to test symbols in experience, to verify them with factual evidence. Thus far, the recent emphasis in education upon science and on mathematics is a good thing.

I am critical of much of what is happening in current curriculum revision. But I do think that most students need to learn how to use the scientific method far more effectively than they do now. If the emphasis on science can teach them to practice its methodology, which is a way of testing ideas in experience, very good. Unfortunately, however, most young people are not learning the scientific method at all well. They are learning something called "science" as formulas, laws, rules, and equations. They are not learning the scientific method as a universal way of analyzing and testing the problems of experience. If they do learn it, they too often place it in a little compartment all by itself, without realizing that the scientific method applies to the whole of nature, not just to little segments of nature.

The result is that many young people graduate from high schools and colleges half scientific and half unscientific. In this assertion I am, perhaps, carrying the practical value of logical analysis farther than the logical analyst himself does. Even so, when he emphasizes a need for setting ideas and symbols up against experiences to make them meaningful, he is fully in accord with the best traditions of scientific thinking and of scientific philosophy. And so another practical implication of our first frontier idea is this: teachers should help young people learn how the scientific method applies, not just to physics or chemistry or biology, but to the whole of life, including personal and social life.

We are reminded here of my earlier comments upon progressivism, and of Dewey's insistence that we have to learn how to use the scientific method in the solution of human problems as well as we have learned to use it in the solution of nonhuman problems. Dewey was not a logical analyst, of course, but on this point there is common ground. Both the progressivist and the logical analyst could contend that we are in danger of destroying ourselves because, although we can use the scientific method to devise atomic bombs, we have not learned how to operate with it in solving moral, political, and economic problems. It is the teacher's first responsibility to help youngsters learn how.

Sociological realism

The second frontier idea, you remember, is sociological realism. Can we help to make this idea, too, more useful? It is an idea that can help us become more realistic about the fact of our socioeconomic position in culture. It implies that our beliefs, the truths and values we cherish, are to a remarkable extent conditioned by the status and the class position in which we find ourselves. This is so even when we are not conscious of such conditioning. Thus it is a corrective to the overlogical stress of the first idea.

Sociological realism has given to me, for one, practical help in understanding my class position in American culture, and in understanding also the role of the schools in the American class structure. Let me try to be as forthright as possible. Through this idea, I have become much more aware of the fact that in many communities our public schools are controlled by small sections of people who do not necessarily speak for the majority interests or values of the community. Studies have been made of the educational structure that lead to much the same conclusion—namely, that the school boards of America are frequently not democratically representative at all. Instead of expressing the interests of a cross section of citizens, they are chosen very often by a small segment of the professional and business classes. Working people are rarely represented on school boards in American communities, even where the majority of the members of that community are "blue-collar" or "white-collar" workers.

And so what happens? Well, of course, the result is that the control of the school rests in the hands of a minority which has its own concerns very much in mind and which therefore encourages the kind of curriculum and the kind of teaching that will promote and solidify its own class and status interests. Yet I am afraid that many teachers in America are not remotely aware of any such pattern of control. They are not aware of it because, for one thing, they have never understood sociological realism.

A further point may be made with regard to the practical implications of this second idea. I have already tried to suggest that it challenges us to think more clearly, not only about what our own class and social position actually is, but also about what it ought to be. In other words, it challenges us to become more aware that life is not neutral and that eventually all of us have to make choices—choices, for example, as to what socioeconomic power pattern we favor and what socioeconomic power pattern we oppose. This conflict confronts us in America, as in every country I have known. The choice between the kind of power pattern you believe in and want to support and fight for and the kind you oppose, do not believe in, and wish to fight against, is crucial indeed to teachers everywhere.

Should you and I, as teachers, have to take sides? Or should we remain neutral with regard to the great power struggles of our day? From my viewpoint, the answer is clear. The choice I have made, the choice that I hope you have made or will make, is in behalf of realignments of power that will advance the democratic values of man toward a world democratic civilization, and against those forces that are blocking such an advancement.

In other writings, I have tried to put it this way: the choice that you and I face, as teachers and citizens, is ultimately between the "forces of contraction" and the "forces of expansion." These are the forces that, on the one hand, retard and limit man's rights, man's authority, and man's power to achieve social-self-realization, and on the other hand, try to advance and spread such human fulfillment across the globe. I am not at all sure, however, that the alternatives lie merely in the foreign policies of the United States and the Soviet Union. Do not interpret me as an apologist for the American status quo; I am not and I have never pretended to be. Although this is not the place to go into detail, I should at least indicate that, in my view, there are many things wrong with our foreign policy. I think that there are at least as many things wrong with the policies of the communist countries. In short, neither of the present major political power structures provides the answer we are seeking for a world democratic civilization in which the forces of expansion would be in control.

But am I being practical at this point? I would like to think so. For what I am saying to my fellow teachers is that we must become political, too. Those who try to tell us that we teachers have no political responsibility, that we ought to keep out of politics, that we ought to separate education from politics, are trying to split us in two. Don't let them do it.

Existentialism

We will pass by the third frontier idea, existentialism, because it will be dealt with in a later discussion of religion and education. Let me anticipate only to this extent: I want to see education become religious. And existentialism has a great contribution to make in this urgent endeavor. Although the task is very practical and very difficult, education should help to generate the quest for a religious quality in life.

Creativity

Let us turn then to the fourth idea, creativity. I have tried to suggest that creativity is characterized by several basic features. One is honesty, authenticity of statement. The artist has, above all, to be honest in expressing himself. However unpopular he is, however unappreciated or misunderstood, his first obligation is to be true to himself, to his materials, to his vision of the world, and to any part of the world that he is attempting to interpret through his art. Another feature of creativity is innovative imagination—that is, originality.

No artist is an artist who merely repeats, merely imitates. Still another feature is insight, the flashes of discovery that the mechanisms of psychoanalysis are only beginning to help us understand. The artist is always a person who is potently unrational in this respect. But his art becomes rational to the degree that he channels his unrational powers through the forms of art in which he is expert.

In the light of these features, what does creativity say that is of everyday importance for us as practicing teachers? It says a tremendous amount. I take special pleasure in turning to this idea because it gives me the opportunity to criticize education today for what seems to be an imbalance away from creativity and toward passivity—toward standardization, toward passing entrance examinations so that one can be sure to get into Harvard University, or Seoul National University, or some other. Even though the examinations may almost totally ignore the qualities of creativity, even though they may avoid the question of whether a young person ought, perhaps, to be admitted to a university because he has potential ability as an artist, nevertheless they continue to dominate and intimidate millions of students every year.

More positively, if education is to become a powerful force in the world of our time, it cannot afford to minimize or subordinate the role of creativity in the experience of learning. The kind of school that pushes art over to the edge of the curriculum, the kind of administrator who says, "Well, if there's room we'll put in a little art, but maybe there isn't room"—such practices and attitudes as these are, in my view, indefensible.

What, then, does creativity contribute to defensible educational practice? Perhaps one way to answer is to apply to the ordinary classroom the dimensions of creativity already mentioned. First, honesty of statement: if we are to encourage young people to be honest with themselves, we have to encourage them also to feel free to express their deepest interests openly and frankly. As long as the teacher poses as an authoritarian ruler, or as long as he or she is more interested in testing the child's ability to remember or to repeat than to express himself in his own ways, this kind of honesty will not occur. The only place that it will occur is in a classroom where both child and teacher feel secure enough, and have a strong enough affirmative relationship, so that both dare to express and to share their own feelings and their own personalities in their own ways.

The atmosphere of mutual respect and integrity, of authenticity and honesty, is really the responsibility of the teacher, first of all. May I dare to say, accordingly, that if any one of you does not really like children, if you find it difficult to feel continuously warm with them, then please do not become a teacher. You only damage them, and yourself, too, if you do.

The second factor in creativity, innovation, also offers many suggestions to educational practice. Yet they all boil down to one mandate: allow room for the learner to deviate, to be different, to create something not quite according to standard. Encourage the learner to do this every time you get the chance.

There are abundant opportunities to turn this suggestion into a practical idea, yet how often do we teachers really try? In overcrowded classes, it is hard to give the individual child enough attention to encourage him to be a unique individual. But even if you have classes of a hundred children, you still have to seek ways to give each child the freedom to create differently, to grow differently, to think differently, and thus to act differently. One practical step toward this goal would be for the school to provide a brief daily place and time for the child—beginning in the kindergarten and coming right on up through secondary school and even the university—to experience freedom from any obligation except to search within himself and to express himself as he sees fit to do so.

The third dimension of creativity, insight, is unlikely to occur unless the first two dimensions are provided for. That is, if we allow learners to be honest with themselves, and if we allow them to be original, insights will more frequently result than if we do not allow these experiences. What is deadly, what destroys insight, is the kind of teaching and learning that compels children merely to absorb rules and skills and subject matters, to meet tests and standards, while allowing no time for the distinctive powers of the learner to emerge. Insight is something you probably cannot directly train. But you can provide room for it to occur more readily than is usual. If a child in a geography course, let us say, is working on a problem, and you encourage him to solve it, and he comes through with a solution that is all his own, you can admire him for it, you can make him feel good about it. In this way, you are nourishing the seedbed for the development of his capacity for insight.

The same rule holds true for the child who is artistic. As I was strolling through a park in Seoul, I came upon an exhibit of children's art. The exhibit began with drawings by very young children and extended all the way to some rather sophisticated sculpture, painting, and other kinds of art by students in high school and perhaps college. At intervals all through that exhibit one could detect evidences of originality, freshness, and honesty, and some of these young artists must also have experienced moments of insight which caused them to create their work in ways that were specific to them alone. I have no doubt indeed, that Koreans are as creative as any people on earth. But the schools have to provide every possible opportunity to encourage this capacity. It is paralyzed when education becomes chiefly a matter of routine learning and examination passing. This is what is deadly to insight.

Social-self-realization

Consider next our fifth frontier, social-self-realization. I have said that here is the guiding star of education. It provides the way to the needed value orientation for our age of crisis—the criterion by which we determine the kind of civilization we want as against the kind we do not want.

How do you bring social-self-realization into the life of the school so that it affects every aspect? The question is not easy to answer, because social-self-realization is so all-pervasive a value. It means, in essence, the ever-growing fulfillment of the powers of man in communion with other men.

The practical significance of this apex value is, I think, that it becomes a kind of measuring stick by which you may judge whether a school is a good school or a bad school. For many years I have carried this measuring stick around in my head. And every time I visit a school anywhere in the world I hold my imaginary gauge up against the classroom procedures, the administration, the curriculum, and the teachers. Because social-self-realization is the supreme good of life, the great goal of life, any school that is not advancing this goal is a bad school, and any school that is advancing it is a good school.

By this standard, I regret to say I have found many bad schools both in America and in other countries—schools that frustrate and block the fulfillment of human capacities, schools that do nothing to encourage young people to grow up to become persons who are creative not only about themselves but about their communities, schools that are so indifferent even to their immediate surroundings that their own grounds are full of weeds and dirt and debris. I have been in classrooms, too, that are so dingy and ugly that if I were a child I would hate to spend a single hour in them. And I have been in classrooms where teachers serve as such strict taskmasters that you sense the sparks of hostility and competitiveness between them and their students the minute you walk through the door.

But, on the other hand, I have been in schools where the quest for social-self-realization is already flowering to a magnificent degree. I wish you could come with me to visit a school near Tokyo, called Tamagawa Gakuen. This private experimental school, which was founded about forty years ago by Dr. Kuniyoshi Obara, is perhaps the best I have seen anywhere in the world. Dr. Obara, one of the three most interesting Japanese leaders whom I have met, deeply believes that children should realize themselves individually and socially to their utmost, yet at the same time learn solidly and fundamentally. As I walked through the art studios, young children at work paid hardly any attention to this gawky, gray-haired American. They were too busy painting lovely screens together, or carving pieces of sculpture for their schoolyards and gardens. In the science laboratories, youngsters were building various kinds of complex instruments, and it was interesting to observe that these learners varied in age from about eight to twelve or thirteen, although they worked together in the same classrooms. Here, moreover, the whole school community is involved in a common endeavor: there are rice paddies, sheep flocks, fish ponds, flower and vegetable gardens, and the students share in caring for all of these as a regular part of their educational responsibilities. Education for social-self-realization is not just an ideal goal at Tamagawa Gakuen: it is a vibrant reality.

Evolution

Evolution, the sixth and last idea discussed in the preceding chapter, is of great practical application to education in at least as many ways as the other five. The one example I choose has the special value, however, of helping to tie together the whole of this discussion. For evolution, as one of the most comprehensive concepts of science ever constructed, also provides a wonderfully fruitful way of uniting into an organic whole the diverse parts of knowledge that make up the curriculum of our typical schools.

To clarify my point, let me cite a definition of evolution by Sir Julian Huxley, perhaps the world's most distinguished authority: "Evolution," he says, "is a natural process of irreversible change which generates novelty, variety, and increase of organization; and all reality can be regarded in one aspect as evolution." Note that Sir Julian does not speak here merely of biological reality, in which Charles Darwin was primarily interested, but of "all reality." Thus we may think of it as encompassing three great levels: the *preorganic*, which includes the astronomical and geological; the *organic*, which of course includes all plant and animal life; and the *postorganic*, which is the level of humanity, with its capacity to think, to plan, to organize its own life culturally.

You see how evolution thus provides an exciting way to integrate all the important subject matters of the school: those of the physical and biological sciences, and those of the behavioral sciences and the humanities. One of the most urgent needs of education is precisely to provide integration for the growing complexity of knowledge. Evolution does just this. Yet, as Sir Julian's definition also implies, it does it so as to open the way to exploration of new experiences (novelty) and diversity of experiences (variety), thereby discouraging the all-too-familiar tendency of education to become routine, dull, and repetitive. The phrase, "increase of organization" suggests, too, the need to unify not only knowledge but all levels of human relations—a need to which these chapters have referred as one of the central problems of our time.

Yet the single most practical contribution that the idea of evolution can make is not so much to the curriculum, though this contribution could be very important, as to attitude. It helps to cultivate an attitude of confidence in every learner and in every teacher. This is implied by the postorganic level of culture; it is the attitude of confidence on the part of human beings that the further development of evolution rests in their own hands, that what they decide to make of their own futures, and how they decide to make it, is no longer something determined by the accidents of genetic mutation. It is determined by the marvelous capacity which only the human being possesses to shape and direct the course of his own destiny.

7/

Education as a High Profession

The question of what the teaching profession is and what it ought to be, and the correlative question of what kind of preparation for teaching is most defensible and desirable, are problems not yet solved, so far as I know, anywhere in the world. Certainly they are not solved in America, where a great deal of heated argument is generated over them. During the last ten years, indeed, there has probably been more widespread disagreement over what constitutes proper qualifications for teaching than ever before.

Some critics contend that most of the time spent on educating teachers is wasted, because they merely acquire a lot of gadgets, a lot of "how-to-do courses," and never really master the subject matters that they supposedly teach. Powerful voices are proclaiming that the teachers' colleges ought to be abolished, or practically abolished, and that teachers ought to be prepared entirely, or almost entirely, in the liberal arts. The need for a few months of teaching methodology is sometimes conceded, but the rest of the time, it is claimed, should be spent in giving the teacher fundamental knowledge of his field.

Many others disagree with this viewpoint, of course. The National Education Association in America, which has some 900,000 members, would not support it. Nor would the so-called educationists—that is, the professional experts in teacher education.

I propose to face the issue in this setting of confusion and disagreement, and to present for critical consideration an effective design for the profession of tomorrow. As I do so, please keep in mind that we shall not be concerned with whether this proposal is practicable or suitable immediately. Of course it is not. But please remember, also, that it is an integral part of the philosophy of education which we have been considering. This philosophy of education is radically democratic and future-ceutered. Therefore, while the proposed design is not necessarily applicable today, it should not be dismissed for this reason. Too many of us in education seem peculiarly prone to shortsighted planning in the name of practicality. Actually, if we are educators worthy of the name, we have to be "impractical" also, impractical in the sense of holding strong commitments and strong objectives as targets toward which we can aim. In our perilous age, only a deliberately audacious design for education is worthy of our profession.

The general point of view from which this design is presented is that of teaching as a high profession. Teachers deserve and should receive a preparation at least equivalent in quality to that available in the best schools of medicine; they must be the equals of the best educated physicians and surgeons.

One might properly inquire: When is a physician so well educated that he is fully qualified to become a member of a hospital staff or to set up his own medical practice? In America, quite a few doctors would doubtless insist that this question has not been adequately answered even by the leading medical schools. At the same time, it is likely that many of the best medical educators would agree upon the four following requirements for every prospective physician or surgeon:

First, he needs a well-rounded, challenging general education. Second, he needs solid, substantial knowledge in the subject area which is most necessary to all practitioners. Third, the physician in training should obtain rich experience in effective practice—that is, in the techniques of medicine. And fourth (here the training of doctors today is probably weakest), he needs to develop a theory of medicine, or, if you wish, a philosophy of the medical arts, in which he comes to understand the contributions of medicine to the growth of civilization. Medical ethics is one of the aspects of this requirement. The history of medicine is another aspect. The nature of scientific method is still another. The fourth requirement, in short, is to provide the doctor with a sophisticated perspective from which he functions, whatever his specialized field of medicine may be.

The requirement of general education

Let me now apply the four basic requirements, by analogy, to the preparation of teachers. General education, as the first requirement, is surely of comparable importance to the two professions. Both teachers and physicians, as servants of the public, are in need of broad acquaintance with the main currents of scientific, social, and other knowledge if they are to relate effectively their specialized roles to the wider whole of human experience.

The problem that remains is the proper nature of general education. In America, at any rate, almost everyone favors some kind or other. But not very many people appear to be certain as to what they mean by the term they are using. Certainly, if I am at all right in the arguments advanced in preceding chapters, general education is not yet successfully provided by the typical liberal-arts curriculum of the typical college or university. And one of the chief troubles is that it is little more than a kind of continuation of high school, by which most of the same subjects are pursued more intensively—foreign languages, science, mathematics, social studies, humanities.

This is not at all what I consider to be effective general education. The kind that is needed, and the kind which some medical educators would probably agree is needed, is really general education. This certainly does not mean a lot of concentrated doses of learning that have little or no discernible relationship to each other. It means, rather, an integrated, organized understanding of the great areas of life and reality which have become necessary to us if we are to function as citizens in our kind of revolutionary world. Still further, it means that general education for the teacher and the doctor, or for anyone else, should consist of large clusters of problem-centered fields of study.

One such cluster would deal with problems of the physical and biological sciences, with constant reference to their significance for the problems for man—for example, atomic energy, its dangers and its promises. While considering these problems, the student of course acquires understanding of the most essential principles of atomic physics. Similarly, he learns biological principles when he studies problems of, let us say, population control. But whatever the problems of science may be, they are brought to bear upon the problems of men.

Here is the guiding purpose of each of the major areas of general education—the great over-arching problems which man must solve if he is to continue evolving, if he is to build the world democratic civilization of which he is now capable. One general area deals with problems of science; another with problems of the arts; still another with problems of communications (here language comes into the picture, but also all the new revolutionary inventions, such as television, that have been developing in the last few years). Lastly, one area deals with problems of economic, political, and social relations, from the interpersonal relations of family members all the way to those of nations.

This kind of integrated general education should include the first two years of the student's college preparation. It should be open to all citizens of average intelligence, whether they are going to be doctors, teachers, farmers, or technicians, and whether or not they plan to end their college studies at the end of the two years. In short, such general education for young citizens of about nineteen and twenty, following graduation from high school, should eventually become universal for average citizens in all countries of the world.

The requirement of behavioral sciences

What I have said thus far is partly recapitulation. Now let us move on to the second of the four major features of education for the profession of teaching. Just as every medical doctor, regardless of his specialty, is expected to know thoroughly the subject matter most necessary to his profession—in his case, the physiological sciences—so every teacher may be expected to know a comparable subject matter.

The teacher, too, is concerned centrally and properly with one phenomenon of nature—in his case, however, the phenomenon of *the behavior of the human being*, both in itself and in its relations to other human beings. This is the universal subject matter of the average teacher, to which all other subject matters are secondary. His primary task is not to teach mathematics or science or history. It is rather to teach human beings how to be human, how to grow into full, rich personalities living in concert with other personalities.

If you agree with me thus far, perhaps you will then agree also that the subject matter necessary for all teachers is best encompassed by the term *behavioral sciences*. The behavioral sciences, sometimes called the human sciences, are those that have to do with the way man, individually and socially, behaves. This is the subject matter that should occupy a block of time proportionate to the time that a physician in preparation studies the physiological sciences.

Let me add a little more about the nature of the behavioral sciences. Many people do not yet seem to realize that four great classes of revolution have occurred in the twentieth century. First are the political revolutions of which so many millions are aware from direct and bloody experience. Second are the revolutions in technology which in turn have produced the revolution in, for example, communication and transportation. Third are the revolutions in the physical sciences which are closely related to those in technology and communications. The fourth class, of which many of us are still only vaguely aware, is the revolution in the behavioral sciences. Within less than a century, and for the first time in history, we have come to the full realization that man can be studied scientifically and controlled scientifically, in the same way as any other object of nature.

Of course, intimations of this revolution go back a long way. It is interesting to note, however, that anthropology is often dated as a science only from 1873; that psychoanalysis was scarcely recognized as a science much before 1920; and that sociology, social psychology, political science, and economics, while they too have much older histories, have only recently attained mature stature as sciences, and thus have only now begun to achieve recognition by the academic world in ways comparable to, say, physics or chemistry.

Along with the maturation of the sciences of man is an even more recent and still only partially recognized event of revolutionary importance. This is the discovery that man is a whole being, and that we must study him as a whole. Thus, while an important place remains for specialized and segmented study, the sciences of man are also becoming interdisciplinary in character. They have to work in close conjunction with each other. And so, to utilize a familiar term, the behavioral sciences also operate on a continuum—an interdisciplinary continuum running all the way from those sciences, such as psychiatry, that deal with the individual ego to those, such as anthropology, sociology, and political science, that deal more often with collective behavior.

Returning now to professional preparation for teaching, we ask: How much time should be devoted to the behavioral sciences? This depends, of course, on how many years of preparation are proposed. As a long-range goal, I propose four additional years after the two years of general education, plus one year of internship. Thus a total of seven years of preparation should be the norm. This is still a little less than that usually required for medical education, but I will settle for it as a perfectly feasible objective when we are ready to recognize that teaching is, or should be, a major profession. Granting that it may take some time to achieve this objective on a wide scale, let us settle for nothing less than a total of seven years. Meanwhile, we can start right away with selected groups and limited numbers, and then expand the numbers.

Under this schedule, about one-half of the four years before internship should be devoted to the behavioral sciences. All teachers should therefore be required to study the major disciplines concerned with the nature of man—some as separate courses, some in close relationship to others. But all should cover just as solidly the relevant subject matters and research as a course on anatomy or neurology covers them in a medical school. Moreover, the behavioral sciences should be so organized as to include many problems of the kind that teachers themselves constantly face: emotional conflicts during adolescent development are one of countless examples.

What, now, about the other two years before internship? One of these years should be devoted primarily to the theory of education, the other to acquiring more thorough familiarity with the subject area or areas in which the teacher plans to function. In considering the latter provision, however, we should make a distinction between the primary and secondary levels. Primary teachers who are in charge of an entire class do not need a major subject except the behavioral sciences. They do need more knowledge of the fields covered by the primary curriculum, such as social studies, language, and mathematics. We should remember that they have already acquired a broad base in general education. But in this third year, more systematic attention should be given to the subject areas according to the level on which they are to be taught. At the same time, some attention should be given to how best to teach them, so that method and content are treated integrally rather than separately.

The secondary teacher who is going to teach only one subject in high school should devote the third year to his field—in conventional terms, the equivalent of about thirty academic hours. This is again, of course, in addition to what he has already acquired in general education. In this proposal, I am not necessarily suggesting that all of his concentrated study occur in one year. If the prospective teacher is sure of the field he wishes to specialize in, some of his work can be taken in other years. But the point is that not less than one-fourth of his time during the four years before internship is concentrated in his special field, remembering that during extensive periods of practice he has further opportunity to work in it. Equally, the primary teacher has opportunity to work in the several fields of subject matter germane to the elementary levels of the schools.[1]

The requirement of practice

The third major requirement of the professional program, you remember, is practice. I have been anticipating this phase of training in referring to the internships which come in the seventh and final year of the teacher's preparation, just as they conclude the entire program of medical education. Here, particularly, I part from my liberal-arts friends. I disagree with their contention that thorough, direct experience in the methodologies of teaching and learning is not important. Some professors of my acquaintance who take this view are atrocious classroom performers. They know almost nothing about how to teach. Too often they assume that giving lectures and requiring examinations that force their poor victims to memorize an avalanche of facts constitute the sum total of their responsibility. As one who was prepared in an academic field and spent several years as a professor in liberal-arts colleges, I may say that I know something of the methods of teaching that are prevalent in higher education. Of course there are superb college teachers, but they are in the minority. The majority are less competent in their methods of teaching than the majority of primary teachers.

When I decided to specialize in educational philosophy and came into close association with educationists for the first time, I learned about a great deal of research and practice in education of which I, no less than others in liberal arts, had been totally oblivious. Certainly there was an abundance of triviality and superficiality, too. But a considerable part was very important and very useful. I believe that what I learned from this association has markedly affected my teaching. I believe, also, that all teachers on every level, including the college level, should be required to engage in extensive supervised practice before they are permitted to assume full responsibility in a classroom, exactly as a doctor is required to do so before he opens his own medical office or performs an operation.

Unfortunately, much of the practice teaching now typical in America is of miserable quality. Many teachers never learn how to practice well, even when they are given classroom experience as apprentices. One trouble is that such practice is postponed too long. While the internship proposal may also suggest postponement, the fact is that rich opportunity to practice should be provided all the way through the seven years. Every student beginning in general education and continuing thereafter ought to become active, for example, in community affairs. And every prospective teacher needs to learn, not merely *about* action, but *through* action—scientific, economic, social, political, and esthetic action—under the leadership of experts who can interpret the significance of what is being experienced.

As students move further and further into their four-year period of work in the behavioral sciences and other areas, practice should increasingly focus upon educational problems. Many of these problems will still be community oriented (for example, family relations), but others will now be school oriented. The school, indeed, is a magnificent laboratory for an almost infinite range of research and involvement which behavioral scientists still largely ignore. (For example, anthropologically it is a fascinating subculture.) It should no longer be ignored within the design for professional education that we are now considering.

The seventh-year internship is, then, not so much a completely new stage of preparation as it is a climax to all the study, the theory and practice, of the preceding six years. It should require full time. The intern should be well paid and he should be constantly supervised by the ablest possible leaders of his own field.

Educational theory for teaching

We return now to the fourth of the major requirements, the equivalent of a year of study of the theory of education, particularly its history and philosophy. Judging once more by analogy with medical education, I fear that this requirement is at present altogether too limited and weak. Many of the courses in educational theory are taught by incompetent instructors, and too often those that are taught are both sterile and divorced from the remainder of the professional curriculum. Moreover, they are rarely related to the kind of practice that I have been proposing.

Yet the fact is that the philosophy of education, always closely related to the history of education and to the other required areas, gives our profession its single most powerful reason for being. It should provide the teacher with clear purpose and dedication. It offers him, if he will accept it, the stamina to endure the hardships that accompany his duties, duties perhaps as arduous as those of any other profession.

In short, the theory of education should, when effective, afford an understanding of the fundamental premises and purposes upon which and for which the whole educational enterprise is built. Moreover, it should enable the teacher to grasp the basic meanings of such terms as education, culture, philosophy—all the concepts and ideals that lead to a consistent, organized, unified point of view toward professional responsibilities, indeed toward his entire lifework. Surely such a requirement is not of secondary importance. Nor should it in any sense be minimized simply because it has been placed fourth in the series of requirements. On the contrary, it is of first importance.

This chapter began with a reference to the controversy in America over teacher education. I have indicated that some powerful groups would like to abolish teachers' colleges almost entirely, while other powerful groups defend the status quo. The position I have taken, however, is neither of these. In common with a few other American educators, I reiterate that the professional education of teachers should attain at least as high a caliber as that of any other profession. With all due respect, we cannot solve the problem by clinging stubbornly even to the better of our teacher education programs of today, any more than we can solve it by replacing them with typical liberal-arts programs.

What should be our strategy, then? How can we carry to fruition a design for teacher education worthy of our high profession? My answer is that we will have to take the offensive by proposing a far stronger and fresher program than any now prevailing. We will frankly concede that our current programs of teacher education are appallingly weak. But, instead of cringing before the pressures of our liberal-arts critics, we will be setting up a much better professional program than any that they themselves propose.

Opportunities already exist to launch pilot programs in teacher education based on the kind of model presented here. Members of liberal-arts faculties, especially from the behavioral sciences, should be invited to cooperate in setting them up. At the same time, by including such colleagues we open up communication and thereby attack one of the barriers between the educationists and the liberal-arts faculties. For, as you surely know, we academicians stereotype each other as badly as other people do, with the result that liberal-arts professors do not really know what the education professors are saying or doing, nor do education professors know the liberal-arts professors much better. Only when both groups are able to join together in a common attack upon common problems will they discover that they have more in common than they thought.

A recent experience of my own at the University of Kyushu in Japan may be of interest here. During a month of lectures sponsored there by the Research Institute of Comparative Education and Culture, I learned that this Institute is made up of a faculty consisting both of educationists and leading members of the liberal-arts faculty—for example, the dean of the school of economics and a professor of psychiatry. These able scholars take education seriously because they have learned about its problems by becoming directly involved in them. The Institute at Kyushu University is a model for many countries to emulate. Indeed, I wish that we had something as promising in the United States to work on the frontiers of education and culture.

You see that it can be done, for it is being done. I urge young people already planning to prepare for teaching to let their voices be heard on this matter. Speak up! Together with citizens and faculty members who recognize the need for change, professional students can help to test experimental designs for teacher education based on the proposal that I have made. Its goal is standards of preparation at least as high as those of any other profession that serves humanity. Do we believe in our profession, too? Then let us not settle for anything less.

Note

[1] The time divisions of this entire model are, of course, to be regarded flexibly. Thus, if in some cases more than a full year of concentrated study in the subject area is desirable, the time allocated for the other requirements could be adjusted accordingly. The model, however, still governs and the balance of parts should remain approximately as suggested.

8/ The Religious Dimension of Education

The preceding chapter, which presented what could be called a normative design for the professional education of teachers, recommended as one of four essential requirements the thorough study of educational theory. So far I have not specified in detail what is meant by the nature of that theory, although these chapters have usually been concerned with it. I propose now to return directly to the requirement of theory and to treat it in terms of one very complex issue—the issue of religion and its relation to education.

As I shall contend more fully in the next chapter, the most neglected theoretical problem in American education today is the problem of values, the problem of purposes, in short, the problem of the good life and the role that education should play in building the good life. This is not the only problem of educational theory, certainly, but it is a crucial one.

That it is likewise of great concern to foreign educators is evident from the fact that South Korea, for example, requires study in the area of moral and character education from the first grade through high school, and that it provides textbooks to make sure that it is taught according to the mandates of its Ministry of Education. I shall note later that moral and character education is also required in Japanese schools, and that the question is of deep concern to Japanese educators. One hears in that country a great deal of discussion of what kind of moral and character education the schools should attempt to teach.

Frequently educators in Japan have also told me that the problem there is more acute than in the United States because my country is thought to be much more religious than Japan is. The implication appears to be that, since we are predominantly a Christian nation, whereas Japan is not only not Christian but is no longer devotedly Buddhist or Shintoist, the need in American schools for moral education is not so urgent.

I disagree emphatically with this opinion of my Japanese friends. America is by no means as religiously vigorous as it once was. But I do agree that historically one finds a close connection between religious life and moral education. In my view, not only is America as much in need of both as are countries like Japan and Korea, but one may question whether any country will meet this need unless the relations of religion and morality and education are examined together.

The background of religion in education

Why is the problem of moral education so difficult in the United States? Let us approach it through the relations of religion to education, bearing in mind that religion usually if not invariably carries profound moral implications. You are aware, I am sure, of a tradition in the United States going back to the founding of our country, which separates the church and the state, and which regards public schools as agencies of the state rather than of the church. Therefore, public-school teachers presumably do not teach a religious doctrine, Christianity or any other.

Because they do not, many private schools have been established under religious auspices—particularly Catholic schools, although one also finds some Jewish and Protestant schools. The main reason for their establishment is that for people of strong religious belief the public schools fail to provide religious indoctrination. Accordingly these private, parochial schools aim to indoctrinate children in the various religious creeds and dogmas of their sponsors, and hence in their own beliefs about morality.

Within the American public school, the separation of church and state has not been complete, however. Thus, until recently my own state of Massachusetts has required children to listen to a reading from the Bible in opening the day's exercises. The question as to whether such a requirement is unconstitutional has now been decided by the Supreme Court of the United States, and I confess to you that I am gratified that its decision outlaws the practice. The public schools have no business indoctrinating any religious doctrine of any sort, even in such a simple way as reading from the Bible or reciting the Lord's Prayer. Yet, many communities regret the decision and even try to violate it in devious ways. We in America remain still very much confused over the whole question of the relation of religion to education and, consequently, of the responsibility of education to morality insofar as a relation exists between morality and religion.

The present situation in American education may also be stated in more theoretical terms. Here I shall apply some of the terminology introduced earlier. You will recall that American philosophies of education have been viewed in terms of two "partnerships": the first, essentialism and perennialism; the second, progressivism and reconstructionism. If we view the problem of religion and education through the framework of these two partnerships, we discover an interesting picture.

The perennialist and essentialist philosophies of education have a long religious tradition behind them. Both draw heavily upon Greek and medieval as well as early modern religion and philosophy. Both are also influenced by Judaic-Christian beliefs about life, destiny, and morality. Consequently the advocates of either the essentialist or perennialist philosophy of education are very frequently people who believe that the ultimate meaning of life and destiny is grounded in the religious doctrines of Western civilization.[1]

And though essentialists and perennialists differ about many things, most of them would probably agree that the religious meaning of life leads to and stems from some kind of absolute Being—a Supreme Being who is called, in practically all languages, God, the Ruler of the universe. Hence, the prime purpose of education is to teach understanding and worship of God. Under the surface of the ethos of Western culture, out of which both perennialism and essentialism grew, one discovers, I think, this common ground in whatever different terms the idea is couched by various philosophers.

The other two American philosophies of education, progressivism and reconstructionism, depart from this tradition. In both of them, again despite many disparities, may be found the belief that man is the director of his own course of life. Thus man himself is also the maker of his own rules, so that whatever rules he establishes—political, economic, physical, or moral—all stem finally from his efforts to provide culture with order, direction, and purpose. Because, then, man is a being who shapes his own course through his own intelligence, the term law acquires very different meaning for the progressivist or reconstructionist than it does for the perennialist or essentialist. A law is not something given to us by some supreme power, whether natural or supernatural. A law is a formulation that men have constructed, often after prolonged effort, in order to operate upon nature—that is, to explain and direct it.

The most familiar religious name for the progressivist position toward law and man's authority over himself is humanism. The progressivist often calls himself a scientific humanist. He believes that humanity continuously makes and reshapes itself; no one or nothing else does this work for humanity. The reconstructionist goes along with this point of view. He, too, is a humanist. But again, as I shall indicate shortly, he differs from the progressivist in certain ways.

If you relate these philosophic orientations to moral education, you at once observe two disparate approaches. One approach assumes that for a person to be moral, to have good character, he must be governed by some final authority grounded in a reality beyond himself to which he can turn for guidance, in which he can wholeheartedly believe, and which provides the standards he needs to give his life security and direction. The "quest for certainty," a phrase made famous by Dewey, is answered for the essentialist and perennialist by a system of preordained law under an absolute lawgiver. Those who have come under the influence of the Judaic-Christian philosophy of religion are already familiar with this kind of belief. To some extent, of course, it is characteristic as well of Oriental religions such as Buddhism in some of its popular forms.

But notice that, according to the second approach, the contention is that if we are to become a moral people, if we are to build a good way of life for ourselves, we shall have to build it primarily through our own struggles, our own aspirations, our own scientific and creative powers. The laws given to us by the great religions are therefore really man's laws hammered out of long and arduous cultural experience.

A familiar example is the Ten Commandments. According to conservative Biblical tradition, God handed down the Ten Commandments to Moses who wrote them on a stone tablet; these became the moral guides which all men were ordered to follow. From the viewpoint, however, of a cultural evolutionist (and both the progressivist and reconstructionist are in certain respects cultural evolutionists), the Ten Commandments are cultural mandates that people shaped together out of many centuries of experience in learning to live together, so as to guarantee in turn the orderly transmission and progression of the culture.

The commandment, "Thou shalt not steal," is a good rule for any culture to have, because if everybody stole from everybody else it would be impossible for people ever to live together in harmony or trust. Laws are an indispensable ally of cultural order, but we know that their meanings and roles change from age to age. Even in the brief history of America, many practices that were once considered legal and moral (the exploitation and destruction of forests is but one example) are now so improper as to be considered forms of theft and therefore illegal and immoral.

And so the question of the kinds of moral education we shall have is closely related to the religious question of the source of law, particularly moral law. The first two philosophies tend to emphasize that the source of moral law is not man, but God. The second two philosophies tend to emphasize that the source of moral law is not God, but man.

In the United States, the debate between these two groups of philosophies under different names and in different formulations continues to go on, year after year, decade after decade, with a good deal of vigor and sometimes bitterness. There are many aspects of the debate, but few if any go deeper than those dealing with the place of religion in education.

The fact, for example, that the essentialist and perennialist philosophies, especially the essentialist, have recently once more come into a period of remarkable influence in American education is not understandable on the surface level where so much of the discussion occurs. Nor is it understandable as long as educational commentators reiterate so tediously that progressivists now find themselves on the defensive and essentialists on the offensive because of the Cold War. Essentialism, we are told, has become popular again mainly because in order to beat Russia we need to train more engineers, more space scientists, more mathematicians. This philosophy, we are also told, offers a better way to victory than does progressivism because it stresses the essentials of disciplined learning.

The contention is superficial. A much more pervasive reason for the swing toward essentialism is that we live in a time of great trouble, and that in such a time it is quite to be expected that many people will turn again to the more habitual and customary ways of providing guidance. These ways always appeal to the insecure, to the fearful, to the past-directed and tradition-minded. Thus the conflict earlier considered, between those who believe that education is primarily transmission and those who believe that education is primarily modification, can now be restated in religious perspective. In every age of crisis, people are torn between the desire to find security in moral sanctions ordained by authority (especially if that authority be absolute and deified) and sanctions that are shaped by man in terms of fresh demands and new institutions.

The resurgence of the essentialist-perennialist partnership is due, at least in substantial part, to the satisfaction that it gives to those who look again toward the former alternative. I have already tried, however, to indicate in various ways that this kind of solution is not the only one available. Rather, granting a temporary loss of ground, the latter alternative, toward which progressivism-reconstructionism points, is far more defensible. This choice is not urgent only in America, of course. But it is urgent in America. Indeed, it is one of the proofs of the fact that my country is itself deeply involved in a crisis that extends across every nation on earth.

The implications of existential humanism

We come then to the reconstructionist approach to the problem of the relations of religion to education. Let us recall that reconstructionism, like progressivism, accepts as far as it goes the religious orientation known as scientific humanism. But now I find it necessary to indicate another departure from, or at least amendment to, the progressivist orientation. You will recall that previous chapters have much too briefly sketched six frontiers of educational theory and practice. One of these frontiers is existentialism. I have not yet attempted to illustrate its practical implications as a frontier of practice.

I propose to do so now by means of an unfamiliar term, *existential humanism*. The reconstructionist philosophy of education, insofar as it is concerned with the problem of a religion in education and therefore with the problem of morality in its relations to religion, is the philosophy of existential humanism.

Many aspects of this problem have not yet been clarified, certainly not by me. If you are intrigued at all by this particular approach, I invite you to ponder upon it much further. Meanwhile, some directions of the needed thinking may be mapped out.

It is necessary first to suggest what existential humanism is opposed to. It is opposed to both the essentialist and perennialist solutions to the problem of religion and morality. In certain respects, it is opposed to the progressivist solution as well. Why is the reconstructionist dissatisfied with the traditional approaches of the first two philosophies? I can reiterate only one dissatisfaction here. These philosophies, I contend, lack faith in man's own concerted strength, in man's own power of intelligence. Therefore, they believe that it is necessary for man to find direction and guidance outside of and beyond himself, in some kind of absolute power usually alleged to exist in a supernatural reality.

Reconstructionists (and progressivists, too) contend, on the contrary, that man has finally matured enough so that he no longer needs to lean upon this kind of extrahuman support, this kind of belief in something beyond himself to which he turns for reassurance in times of abnormal stress. As I tried to suggest in talking about evolution as one of the great theoretical frontiers, man is the evolution-directing animal, the only one on earth. But if he is ever to grow up all the way, to become a mature being who believes in his own capacity to channel his own evolutionary course, he is going to have to face the fact that he and his fellow men must decide ultimately on what direction they want such a course to take.

In this time of anxiety, human beings are the ones, the only ones on earth, who are able to choose whether we wish to destroy ourselves or to renew ourselves, to make ourselves over again into a far greater civilization than history has ever known. Here, then, is the key to my objection to traditional philosophies: ultimately, despite all their elaborate rationalizations. they lack profound faith in man. They think that we human beings have always to turn to some source of authority other than ourselves, some other power presumably greater than ourselves. From my viewpoint, this is really a mark of cultural adolescence rather than cultural adulthood. It suggests that man, like the adolescent, is still dependent upon someone or something else for his most important decisions and actions.

Let us next consider a reason or two for regarding progressivism as inadequate in its treatment of religion and education. Much as one may sympathize with progressivism, it remains weak in at least two qualities—qualities through which existential humanism, I hope, invites us to be strong.

First, progressivism, as mentioned earlier, has remained too largely a philosophy of means, of methods, of processes. It has not remained entirely so, of course. It is concerned with ends, too. But the emphasis in the progressivist philosophy is on "how" more often than on "what," on process more often than product, on means more often than on ends. This is one objection. A philosophy of education that is going to cope effectively with our crisis age must be a philosophy committed to ends as well as to means, to strong ends, strong purposes, strong goals which we can fight for because we believe in them with all our hearts as well as all with all our minds. Progressivism fails to supply this requirement.

The second lack is that progressivism in broadest perspective remains an anthropocentric philosophy. That is, it too easily sloughs off the fact that man is, after all, but a minute segment of the universe.

Or may I put it differently? Progressivism is too often relatively indifferent to the mystery of existence, and hence to the ultimate mystery both of the human being and of the cosmos itself. Again I recognize that the great philosophers of pragmatism and progressivism by no means ignore these concerns. But their focus of attention is not on the existential dimension of man and nature; it is rather on the scientific, practical processes by which man understands and controls man and nature. The emphasis is rationalistic, the emphasis is instrumental, the emphasis is on intelligent direction of man and nature. Progressivism is not greatly troubled with the mysterious yet immediate existences that precede man and follow man. In short, progressivism and the philosophy behind it—pragmatism or experimentalism—are insufficiently existential.

The existentialist, therefore, has something additional and important to tell us that strengthens our sense of identity. By deepening human meaning, we become in turn not less but more human than we were before. And so, let me try to restate very briefly the kind of orientation toward man and the universe that this philosophy seeks to grasp.

A previous chapter pointed out that although existentialism is primarily a European philosophy it is beginning to exert considerable influence on American culture—especially on religious thinking but even on such fields as the philosophy of education. Because existentialism, however, is more a mood than a systematic theory, it becomes exceedingly difficult to define in the way that one might define, say, objective idealism or dialectical materialism.

Nevertheless, one detects a common quality in the mood of all existentialists. This common quality centers in an awareness that man is ultimately and finally an existent self, a self that lies beneath rational and scientific analyses and that is yet involved with the whole of existence.

One also detects something very unrational about this mood—so much so that we are not surprised to hear these days of a new school of psychiatry called existential psychoanalysis. Freud himself, or at least part of his theory, is claimed by this school. Its exponents, although they too differ among themselves, agree that the self can never be grasped either by itself or by others until its own fundamental existence is somehow recognized. And yet, each of us must try to understand and control our own selves as far as we possibly can even while confessing that complete success is never forthcoming.

The fact, moreover, that we never succeed fully in grasping the meaning of our existence is a major source of anxicty. According to the existential psychoanalyst, anxiety rests primarily in the ultimate impossibility of explaining either ourselves or the non-philosophical, unrational existence of the universe. To be sure, we are able to understand the universe increasingly through astronomy and physics. Yet think for a moment of how little we really know about the universe even in astronomical terms. For example, we do not know for sure whether life is to be found on any other planet. Scientists guess that probably millions of planets are able to sustain life. Thus far, however, not a shred of direct evidence is available to them that this is true.

And just as the existence, much less the scientific character, of life beyond the earth remains enshrouded in mystery, so does the even more ultimate mystery of death. Aristotle said that all men are mortal, hence that no man is ever immortal. We all die, and to a greater or lesser extent we are all afraid of death. Thus, consciously or not, we become anxious, because we cannot avoid awareness of what the existentialist may call the terrifying inevitability of nonbeing, emptiness, nothingness.

In our age of threatened destruction, itself fraught with even more than average anxiety over life and death, we hear the existentialist speaking to us about the ultimate agony of being human. And this is what I really mean by existential humanism. We are all members of humanity. We possess enormous though largely latent powers as human beings to improve our lot by controlling nature and human nature. The progressivist is thus far right about his humanism. But we are also beings who must face the fact of existence and pay the price of anxiety and dread in facing it.

What practical significance does existential humanism have for us as teachers? And how can we relate this point of view to the problems of teaching morality and religion in the schools? These are big questions and again I do not begin to know all the answers. May I, however, offer two suggestions? First, the public schools need to study, really study, the great religious approaches to life and the universe—Oriental, Occidental, humanistic, theistic—all the major ones. Second, the existential humanist point of view should be considered comparatively and critically along with the others.

This is not at all to say that we ought to indoctrinate this point of view. I am against indoctrination of every kind—political, religious, or any other. Public schools have no business indoctrinating anything. But I do favor studying the religions of world cultures sympathetically and thoroughly, both as great historical movements and as powerful moral beacons. One of these moral beacons, I increasingly believe, is existential humanism. For what it does, in a sense, is to create a healthy moral paradox, a strong belief both in legitimate human hope and power and in the limitations that existence places inexorably upon every human hope and power. Maximum awareness of each element of the paradox strengthens the other element, and thereby strengthens humanity by strengthening its image of itself.

Out of the debate of comparison, evidence, criticism, and argument, let students and teachers arrive at their own free agreements or disagreements as to which, if any, of the major religious philosophies offers them the most help and the richest promise. In the atmosphere of this kind of free and open learning, perhaps some students and some teachers will arrive at something like the existential humanist position.

I do not know for sure. But I am willing to conjecture that, were we to give this philosophy of religion, morality, and education a fair and thorough hearing, a great many people would come to recognize that it is a position perhaps much more defensible than some of the other religious philosophies which continue to exercise such sway over Western and Eastern cultures.

Note

[1] The qualifying term, "very frequently," suggests exceptions, the most important being the "realist essentialists" who are the heirs of such philosophers of modern history as John Locke.

9/

Values: Education's Most Neglected Problem

Accompany me, please, to a rural junior high school which I recently visited. Here, in a very crowded classroom, are fifty boys and girls averaging about fourteen years of age. They are seated around tables at each of which a student is leading a lively discussion. The male teacher is moving busily from table to table, offering suggestions, clarifying questions, encouraging disputation. Neither the boys, who are in rather stern navy blue uniforms with brass buttons, nor the girls, who are in middy blouses and blue skirts, pay much attention to their visitors. They seem totally engrossed in their discussion. Even when I take a flash picture, only two or three look toward me.

I prize that picture, not only because I am possibly the world's worst photographer and this happens to be a miraculously good one, but because you and I would have a great deal of trouble finding in the United States a single junior high school or, for that matter, any public school on any level, where anything like the same kind of learning experience is taking place. For what we were observing was a program centering in the study of values. The place: a coal mining community on the Island of Kyushu in western Japan.

The program is required of all students, but it was apparent to me that here was one requirement, at least, which they thoroughly relished. The questions they considered were not remote from their experience, nor were the answers preformed by the faculty in the way that answers to chemistry and arithmetic problems might be. The issue with which the class was concerned during my visit involved the sharing of responsibility—a value-laden term itself—among the fifteen hundred students. It could well have been the responsibility of maintaining the beautiful flower gardens which they themselves had planted in the school yard.

I wish I might have stayed long enough to discover whether the class finally resolved the specific issue of that day and what policy they may then have recommended for school-wide adoption. But I was soon conducted to a room in the library in order that the principal could show me another remarkable feature of his school. There, lining the walls on all four sides from floor to ceiling were hundreds and hundreds of neatly bound documents prepared by students and teachers of many classes in what the school called "moral education." Each document was a case study of some problem that had been considered. The whole collection was a record of the ten or more years that this program had been in active operation.

The studies all relate, I was told, to the lives of the young people who worked at developing them. Sometimes the students dealt with school problems—discipline, say; at other times they reached out to their families and to the economic and political troubles which seem to be just as rife in coal mining towns of Japan as in those of the United States. The documents are often consulted by subsequent classes, who try thereby to learn from past experience in coping with present and future problems. I believe I recall also that the ethics library of this school is frequently consulted by other junior high schools which are not yet as far along in their programs of moral education.

A visiting observer of Japanese education is bound to inquire into the reasons for so remarkable a venture. He wonders why that country seems to be so much more engrossed in the question of the proper role of values in its school program than is our own. As I traveled from the northern to the southern end of Japan and talked with dozens of university presidents, professors of education and philosophy, principals, and leaders of the powerful teachers' union, I found them to be genuinely troubled about the program. It is now required by the Ministry of Education not only in the elementary and junior high schools, but now, for the first time since the end of World War II, in the senior high schools as well. What they fear, of course, is that the federally controlled curriculum of Japan will lead to indoctrination of ethical principles congenial to the presently conservative political regime. They remember too painfully the prewar years when children were indoctrinated with emperor worship and the "virtues" of military might. It is not surprising, then, that the teachers' union has militantly opposed all official efforts to require "moral education."

I do not doubt that this opposition, supported by many university professors, influences the character of the present program so that, as in the example just described to you, students are encouraged freely to examine and clarify their ethical judgments rather than to accept the preconceived judgments of those in authority. Likewise, the new senior high-school requirement centers in comparative study of some of the great moral thinkers of all time, from Socrates to Confucius to Dewey, together with application of their ideas to contemporary situations in Japanese life.

Reasons for the continuous stream of debate about the place of ethics and the study of values in the education of this remarkable country are not found, however, merely in its unfortunate past record. A more pervasive reason is that Japan is passing through the most revolutionary period of transformation in its history, a period which began with the Meiji regime scarcely a century ago but which has since accelerated at breathtaking speed. Such a transformation, which as you know has already brought Japan close to the forefront of the world's industrial powers, penetrates every segment of its culture—including, of course, its magnificent traditional arts, its gracious family patterns, its religious customs, and certainly its moral habits and principles. Even superficial acquaintance with Japanese life reveals the often traumatic effects of this upheaval—an upheaval compounded by the terrible devastation of World War II. Millions of citizens are bewildered by the disintegration of older standards and the immaturity or evasiveness of newer ones. In this atmosphere of groping and anxiety, issues centering in values quite suddenly become much more than academic curiosities. They become issues of poignant personal and social urgency.

No wonder, then, that the educators with whom I discussed the matter all showed, though not always in words, their awareness that the way of dealing with moral education could have tremendous effect either for evil or for good upon the entire future of their culture. It was because of this awareness that they so often asked me for any help that I might be able to give. "Tell us," they would plead, "how do you study ethical questions in your American public schools? We have learned widely from you in other ways. We have borrowed heavily from your technology. We have admired many of your art forms. Much of our school curriculum is modeled upon your own. How, then, shall we teach values?"

You can, I am sure, appreciate my embarrassment as I heard such questions. I had to reply that moral education in the United States is practically nonexistent in any direct sense except within our parochial schools. And in these, unfortunately, it is almost exclusively taught as indoctrination according to the absolutist theologies of the churches that control their policies. I did point out that now and then a handful of public and private schools have tried experimental projects in the study of values and that able research studies have recently been made of the ethical attitudes of teachers and students. Still, I could offer little real advice to my Japanese colleagues based upon American practice. Rather I could have confessed that, in my country, values are education's most neglected problem.

Yet had I been asked I might at least have tried to explain why. Perhaps it is just as well that I was not asked, however, for the answer as I have thought about it since has many aspects. Why is the study of values education's most neglected problem? Let me select four of many possible dimensions of the answer to that question.

Factors in the neglect of values

First, as its ecclesiastic critics often contend, the secularization of public education certainly shares responsibility. A curriculum which concentrates on so-called objective knowledge and skills safeguards most teachers from trespassing deliberately upon the precarious territory of values and value judgments. Thus, teachers are safeguarded also from charges of involvement in controversial issues, which of course are saturated with ethical implications.

In the past few years, moreover, the trend toward subject-centered learning, fact-acquiring study, and skill mastering has, if anything, expanded both with the demand for technically trained personnel and the pressures to pass objective examinations for entrance to college. It could be proved, I think, that this expansion of so-called subject-matter curricula is in something like inverse ratio to the contraction of direct educational concern with problems of ethical behavior. And teaching machines only encourage the trend. It is hard to imagine a machine that would enable young people to resolve lively moral issues. Let us pray that, when I next visit the same junior high school in Japan, I shall not find fifty teen-agers frantically pressing buttons for the right answers to their ethical dilemmas.

A second reason for our relative indifference is more fundamental and helps further to clarify the first reason. It centers in a profound disparity between the recent history of modern Japan and that of the United States. Whereas the transformation of Japan occurs almost before one's eyes, the industrial evolution of the United States has been steadier, less disruptive of the political, social, and economic structure. Still more important, the people of the United States have only once known the ravages of war within their own borders, and they have never suffered invasion by an outside enemy. By contrast, the Japanese people, the first and only people thus far in history to experience atomic bombing, suffered perhaps more horribly than any single victim of the war.

No wonder that even today a visitor to Japan is struck by the frequency with which almost all important events are dated in conversation by the phrases "before the war" or "after the war." The fact that one rarely hears an American using either phrase in conversation is, I think, symptomatic of two disparate cultural moods. While World War II certainly left its scars upon us also, we have been much quicker to forget. By the same token, most of us have refused to believe very seriously that America, too, is caught in the meshes of the same planet-wide revolutions, the same unprecedented crises, that now compel the Japanese to search freshly and deeply for their own cultural identity, for reformulated national goals, and for new forms of cultural dynamics by which these goals may be obtained.

Thus, despite our current salutary disturbances of conscience over the disgraceful treatment of Negro fellow citizens, the commonest critique of ourselves by a wide range of competent interpreters both here and abroad is that we are still an apathetic people—a people more concerned to conform than to deviate or dissent. We are still mainly preoccupied with winning the approval of our peers according to the prevailing mores of suburbia and middle-class society. We are still sure of our long-range technological superiority. Most of us are still confident that in a show-down we can win again in the power struggle of nations.

The consequence, of course, is that conflicts of value, which in fact are inherent in any serious questioning of such prevalent attitudes, rarely rise to the surface of wide public concern. On the contrary, if we test this contention by the degree to which education reflects any such concern in its usual courses of study, we discover very little indeed. As I have noted in my discussion of secularization as the first reason for neglect of value problems in education, one observes, if anything, less rather than more concern today than twenty years ago. For the pendulum still continues to swing further and further away from child-centered, community-centered, or problem-centered programs of learning, and closer and closer toward tightly organized subject-matter programs, efficiently taught by methodologies that resemble nothing so much as the technologies that they are designed primarily to serve.

A third reason for our neglect of the value problem centers in the teaching profession and is, like the first reason, largely an effect of the cultural situation which I have been discussing. A conforming curriculum is surely the product of a conforming culture. But so, too, are conforming teachers. A curriculum that would deal competently with values requires deeply concerned and informed teachers, who, after all, are responsible for dealing with values, if anybody is. By this gauge, and granting many exceptions, I question whether American teachers are as competent as Japanese teachers. For, despite their poorer educational equipment, much lower salaries, larger classes, and longer workdays, my observation is that the members of the teaching profession in that country are more alert to its rightful influence over the policies of education, more politically sophisticated, and less easily intimidated by pressure groups than is the rank and file of American teachers. The explanation, moreover, is surely in part that our fellow teachers of Japan are closer to the revolutions of our age, more involved in the conflicts that generate revolution, and much more aware of the dreadful possibility of human annihilation than most of us are. And so they are readier than we to bring into their classrooms the cultural troubles that so often come to focus in moral considerations.

On at least one score, however, it is likely that the teaching professions of both countries are equally incompetent. I therefore reiterate a contention stressed in a preceding chapter: most professional schools of education neglect foundational work in two areas, philosophy and the behavioral sciences, that could enable teachers to deal with value problems in informed and therefore professional ways. If we limit philosophy only to the division of that field most germane to our interest here—namely, axiology, the study of value theory—who can deny that the great majority of teachers in either country have almost no acquaintance with the chief points of view prevailing among philosophers today? Yet, unless they do have some acquaintance, I fail to see how the ethical complexities arising on the practical level of everyday life can be effectively handled at all.

The behavioral sciences are indispensable, also, to the preparation of qualified teachers. They enable teachers to approach axiological issues in a context of knowledge about the way man, and therefore the student himself, behaves individually and socially. To raise problems of value without this context is to treat them abstractly and bloodlessly. To set them in this context provides teachers with the resources of a working partnership between philosophy and the behavioral sciences which could be of boundless benefit not only in building professional competence but, of far more importance, in making possible the kind of teaching and learning that deals with values as the living stuff of real human beings. Thus far, however, the behavioral sciences, with the exception of one, psychology, receive only minimal attention in the typical programs of teacher education in America.

The fourth and final factor that I select to account for our neglect of values in public-school study—namely, limited experimentation and innovation—is the consequence of the other three. Education which (1) maximizes the mastery of fixed subject matters and minimizes the human problems of our crisis civilization, (2) reinforces the complacency and apathy so chronic in the American mood of our day, and (3) fails to prepare most teachers at all adequately in the very areas most vital to their cultural effectiveness—such an education is surely not likely to engage in many innovations that would seriously disturb conventional curricula or to test experimental projects in the domain either of value criticism or value creation.

I am saying that there is very little exciting experimentation going on in American education today, and least of all in such areas as bear upon issues of values. This is not to say that no experimentation is taking place in the public schools. In largest part, however, the kinds that do take place are geared to improving the efficiency of instruction, to the updating of subject matters such as chemistry or physics, and to advancing intellectually gifted students at more rapid rates. We need not be at all surprised that the social studies are among the last of the major fields to receive renewed attention, nor that most of the proposals for their improvement are pathetically timid, unimaginative, and confused by murky purposes.

I wish now to pay further attention to the third and fourth obstacles that block effective value study, but I shall try to do so in more constructive ways. Let us therefore consider two questions.

The first: What is necessary in the preparation of teachers in order that they may be more qualified than most are at present to cope with problems of values?

The second: What kinds of curricular innovations may be suggested by which these problems may be explored effectively in the public schools?

Insofar as we act upon our answers to both questions, we shall have begun to reverse the swing of the educational pendulum once more. We shall have begun to re-create the kind of learning dedicated to the most crucial of all responsibilities in public education, that of developing citizens thoroughly aware of the deepest problems of national and world culture, citizens therefore confident of their own capacities to attack these problems with intelligent, concerted power in behalf of their most compelling goals.

Values in the education of teachers

How shall we answer the first of our two questions? The steady attack upon teacher education for its superficiality and busywork is in my view very much justified. What is not justified is the corollary that virtually all professional education for teachers should be abolished and replaced by far more intensive work in the liberal arts. Earlier I have made proposals for the rebuilding of teacher education on a level of excellence equal to that of education for such professions as medicine and law. Here I can only reemphasize two requisites: there must be thorough grounding in both philosophy and the behavioral sciences.

Among the behavioral sciences, the most neglected one, anthropology, could easily become, ironically, the most useful of all. I say "could" because, no less than other fields, anthropology is sometimes taught in so sterile and dull a fashion as to have little impact upon any learner, including prospective teachers. The kind of anthropology I have in mind, moreover, is not sharply separated from other sciences of man. It is the most encompassing of these sciences, for its demarcating theme is the nature of culture. Anthropology is thus bound to be concerned sooner or later with such relations as that of personality structure to cultural patterns and therefore of psychiatric behavior to cultural behavior. Still more relevantly, anthropology cannot ignore (even though too many anthropologists try their best to do so) the significance of education interpreted as a process quite as much a part of culture as is religious life. Above all, in terms of our interest here, anthropology more and more zealously investigates the function of values in cultural experience. And while, as a science, it is properly chary of prescriptive judgment about the values it observes, at least it no longer avoids careful descriptions of their nature, and sometimes it ventures still further into normative considerations of paramount importance.

I have chosen anthropology for emphasis, but it is not my intention to depreciate the importance of other behavioral sciences in the needed new programs for prospective teachers. In another relatively neglected field, psychiatry, the function of values is equally prominent. So, too, in fields such as political science and social psychology. But I return to anthropology because it affords perhaps our best opportunity to underscore the need for new interdisciplinary approaches to problems of human life. Granted that there will always be an important place for specialists in personal and social behavior, it is also true that few of the problems faced by children and adults are completely separable into components such as the psychological or political. Like the human being himself, most of these problems are an intricate Gestalt, a "field of forces" that are subjective and objective, emotional, rational, and cultural. So, equally, are the problems of value that interweave throughout the Gestalt.

Philosophy, too, is now beginning to be recognized again as a coordinative rather than a purely self-sufficient discipline. After a period in which the proponents of logical analysis have tried to rule the philosophical roost, we are finding, for example, that some behavioral scientists work closely with philosophers on matters of common concern. So, too, an increasing number of colleges of teacher education are establishing strong programs called educational foundations. These bring together in mutual interest not only philosophers and historians but estheticians, psychologists, sociologists, and even an occasional anthropologist. In this development, indeed, these colleges are well ahead of colleges of liberal arts, most of which resist any change in their proud proliferation of atomized subject matters and sovereign departments.

The Achilles heel of cross-disciplinary studies is, of course, the familiar one of breadth at the expense of depth. Although I recognize that breadth and depth are both essential, I wish to look now at the special need for fundamental study in depth of axiological problems without which we cannot hope to deal effectively with problems of value in education. One might well question, for example, whether the classes in "moral education" now required in the Japanese public schools are usually conducted by teachers qualified to recognize the variety of value theories about which philosophers now eagerly dispute. The largely unresolved difficulty here is similar to that in other relevant fields such as psychiatry: Can we provide the teacher with enough familiarity with axiological theory so that he effectively applies those theories on the plane of practice? We should recognize that he is not, after all, a professional philosopher and cannot be expected to perform as one.

At least one carefully planned and solid course in axiology is the minimum requirement for all teachers in preparation. The course should include abundant case studies, drawn wherever possible from actual experience, to illustrate how axiologists of different persuasions approach live options of value. In such a course, students would not only be sensitized to classical theories that still exercise prodigious influence in practical affairs—the teleological, utilitarian, evolutionary, instrumentalist, Thomist, personalist, Zen Buddhist, Marxist, and others—but they would come to terms with the most recent thinking in the field of axiology. For example, they would consider the intriguing distinction between metaethics and ethics proper—that is, the distinction between the psychological, social, or other grounds of ethics and the normative principles or standards that rest upon those grounds. Again, they would have to become aware of the contentions of the still powerful supporters of logical analysis, many of whom contend that value judgments are incapable either of logical or scientific validation. And they would be able to detect the existentialist mood in its approach to values when they found it in actual behavior—the mood that usually grounds value in pure, unrational subjectivity, and insists upon the supremacy of human freedom only when thus grounded.

In suggesting that the axiological preparation of teachers should encompass major philosophic approaches to value problems, I do not mean that it should be limited to a merely eclectic survey. Those who teach axiology usually have a point of view of their own, which is their right. This should be made plain to the student, but he should also be confronted with the hard and fair competition of other points of view. As far as possible, without either manipulation or coercion, students should seek consensus as to their agreement or disagreement with the axiological position that the course espouses.

To illustrate personally, it happens that I support a naturalistic and humanistic philosophy of values—a philosophy earlier epitomized by the frontier concept of social-self-realization. I hold also that values may be just as amenable to scientific study and testing as any other phenomenon in nature. Indeed, this is one of the reasons why we should welcome close philosophic cooperation with behavioral scientists in their recent commendable research into the values of personal and cultural life.

Moreover, I am supported by philosophers like John Dewey and psychologists like Abraham Maslow in contending that the hoary dichotomy between descriptions of value and prescriptive choices among values is no longer unbridgeable. I have even tried to suggest that the way to build a bridge is by what may be called consensual validation. This is admittedly a complex and insufficiently defined process, to be sure, but one which has the advantage of considerable testability in classrooms as well as in communities. By consensual validation, in briefest terms, I mean a process by which I first express to others one or more of my own value preferences, each of which I define as a want-satisfaction. I express these preferences in the richest possible dialectic of cooperative, open, searching examination. In this process I also seek from others their own evidence and reasons for sharing or not sharing in my preferences. We then try to achieve whatever agreements or disagreements we can together, with a view to actions that will overtly dramatize our judgments and thereby help to check them.

Perhaps this sort of theory lies behind the Japanese program that I described to you, although how far teachers or principals would express their underlying theories in terms similar to mine, or how far they are aware of alternative theories that should also be presented for application to problems the students confront, I am unable to say. I do say that the study of values by children even below junior high-school age is not impracticable according to the theory I support. I also say that one of the greatest difficulties in translating this theory from merely verbal formulation to classroom practice is that of internalization: teachers must be enabled to perceive and to act so that theories become operating concepts which, when applied, can make a prodigious difference in everyday performance.

Curricular innovation in values

The preceding statement leads directly to our second question. Let me rephrase it: How do you actually begin to make changes in the curriculum of the public schools so that problems of value receive the serious attention that they rightly require?

Several promising ways deserve consideration, but the one that may occur to us first should be looked upon with skepticism. This is the suggestion that although values are of course indispensable to education—who would deny that?—the best assurance of dealing with them in the classrooms is to provide due attention to them in regular courses of study. This is sometimes called the "indirect" approach. According to this approach, teachers should encourage students in literature, for example, to become aware of the values that abound in that field—friendship, love, service, sacrifice, and courage, to name a few. Esthetic values in the arts, social values in history, economic values in business and labor, even the values inherent in scientific research such as the love for truth—all of these and innumerable others should be made more explicit than they usually are in regular eourses of study.

This approach is defective on several grounds. As some of us have discovered as we try to work in the field of human-relations education, the "indirect" approach frequently means that nothing very much happens at all. At least until teachers are much better qualified in philosophy and the behavioral sciences than they are at present, the likelihood is that, when the task is left to their individual discretion, most of them will avoid deliberate considerations of value, except very incidentally. I emphasize "deliberate," however, because no teacher can entirely avoid such considerations. Values, fortunately or unfortunately, not only have a way of infiltrating virtually every facet of the curriculum, but teachers have the habit of conveying value jugments to learners even when they are unaware that this is what they are doing.

One might legitimately contend that a conscious attempt to articulate values in regular courses would be an improvement at least over what is now common practice. The difficulty remains, however, that conscious attention does not necessarily mean critical attention. On the contrary, the explication of values in a field such as literature could amount to nothing more than a reinforcement of customary value orientations that may or may not deserve reinforcement. This is particularly likely when the values that are noted—friendship or courage are good enough examples—are so general and agreeable that they conceal the complex and conflicting meanings that real situations frequently generate.

One need not, to be sure, contend that the indirect approach would always be unsatisfactory. Teachers well prepared to deal with value problems should certainly raise them whenever they can, indirectly as well as directly. With my Japanese colleagues, however, I contend that direct approaches to value problems are indispensable. Otherwise the whole obligation is sure to be deferred or avoided, just as it is now.

One direct approach with which I have had some personal association is in the form of a series of projects that may be considered for eventual testing by the Ethical Culture Society. The Society operates excellent private schools which are notable, among other reasons, for the deliberate study of ethics on the secondary level. An academic quartet consisting of Professors Joseph Blan, Philip Phenix, and Goodwin Watson of Columbia University, and myself were requested by the Society to reexamine the whole question of how ethics could best be vitalized in teaching and learning.

Our proposal is that experimental projects be attempted in five related areas: conservation of natural resources, the class structure, sexual morality, religion, and world government. As we developed each of these areas, the conflicting axiologies which I have already urged as a requirement for teacher education were often sharply debated among the four of us. Nevertheless, emerging from our efforts is a whole series of proposals to deal with each of the five areas by means of consciously chosen issues of value. Sex education, for example, is not for us primarily a matter of instruction in the physiology of reproduction, as it still is today in most schools that deal with sex at all. Rather, we saw it in its proper light—that is, as primarily a moral question, and a very distressing one for young people of this generation. Again, in dealing with conservation of natural resources, we realized not only that *conservation* is a value term in and of itself, but that the questions it raises are complex indeed: conservation of what resources, conservation for whose benefit? The class structure raises equally thorny questions: Where should one attach one's social loyalties—with the upper classes, say? Or the middle classes or the lower classes, or perhaps with none of these? The value implications of religious experience are perhaps even more obvious than those of conservation or class, but not for this reason are they less disturbing. Our group was, I think, in general agreement that the great religions should be critically studied in all public schools, with particular regard for their ethical dimensions, and of course without the indoctrinating practices now happily outlawed by the Supreme Court. The fifth area, world government, I shall leave for later comment. The central point I wish to make, meanwhile, is that the common denominator of all five areas as we propose to study them experimentally is the critical study of values, which make up a delicate and intricate fabric that clothes every area with meaning and challenge for learners on the threshold of maturity.

Still another proposal, one that combines, perhaps, some of the indirect approaches with the direct, is an experimental project that has been conducted under my direction in the Lexington, Massachusetts, senior high school. Stimulated by a seminar on possible ways to study the elusive concept of mankind in the public schools, a team of three doctoral candidates in the philosophy of education at Boston University, Charles Clayman, Thomas Dodge, and Richard Lyons, developed a program for junior and senior students of the social studies. The central theme of the project was this: How far are we, young citizens of an American middle-class subculture, different from and similar to people of very different cultures in other parts of the world?

In seeking to answer this question, both the teaching team and the students planned a good deal together. They entered vicariously into two distant cultures (one in the South Seas, one in India) by means of research materials provided by anthropologists. They spent time associating closely with the Negro community of Boston. On several occasions, they brought visiting authorities into the classroom. They reached back over two thousand years into history to learn something of the cultural patterns and the ethos of the Athens that Socrates knew.

As the work progressed, it was fascinating to me as a "participant observer" in the project to note how frequently the term values entered into the class discussion of these youngsters seventeen and eighteen years old, and how they grew in their perceptiveness of such a well-worn but far from worn-out issue as "relative versus universal values."

On both occasions that the project has been conducted over a period of some twelve weeks, the evidence shows that most students become significantly more conscious of their own values in relation to those of others. Nor do I exaggerate in asserting that many saw themselves clearly for the first time as members of one human race. The human race has great disparities, to be sure, but also surprisingly common problems and common aspirations.

The Lexington project brings me back to the problem of world government and world order—the last of the areas, you remember, considered by our Ethical Culture group. Although I shall develop this problem more fully in the concluding chapter, the point to be underscored now is that we are dealing here with a question fraught with both profound value conflicts and crucial value choices. Actually, most Americans have not yet faced fairly and unequivocally either the ethical conflicts or the choices involved. The issue is not, if we think about it at all, one that can be decided by political science alone or by any other science. It has to be decided on the basis of our most authentic human purposes. Are we to continue to seek their achievement through competition, national rivalry, hatred, suspicion, prejudice, and force, or are we to seek it through the evolutionary principle of human convergence? If the former, let us at least be clear that this is what we want. If the latter, let us face the necessity for radically new economic arrangements assuring equitable distribution and democratic control of resources throughout the planet. Let us endorse, also, an enforceable system of democratic international authority, both to guarantee this distribution and to prevent the ruinous and probably final war which is almost sure to be the alternative to this kind of authority.

I therefore conclude this chapter with a plea for the axiologizing of public education as a whole. The time indeed is already well passed when we can afford to indulge in the luxury of cluttered curriculums, in spurious academic aloofness rationalized in the name of objectivity, in confused if not often obsolete codes of moral conduct, and in stultifying ambitions to grasp the dubious goals of success and status at whatever cost to our personal and communal integrity. For the grim truth is that nothing less than the life of mankind as a whole is now in precarious balance. To reassert that values are education's most neglected problem is really to insist, with our Japanese brothers, that we no longer have any genuine choice—no choice but to bring the nature and meaning of values out of the shadowy background and into the spotlight of sustained concern on every level of learning from kindergarten through the university.

10/

World Civilization: The Galvanizing Purpose of Public Education

"We see our fundamental goal as a world civilization and an educational system which in all ways support human dignity for all races, castes, and classes; self-realization; and the fullest vocational, civic, and social cooperation and service. In achieving this fundamental goal, there must be understanding of and commitment to the proposition that education is a primary instrument of social change and social welfare."

This statement was not written by a group of starry-eyed educational theorists. It was not prepared by one of the many feeble little groups in America who promote some form of internationalism. It was written and subscribed to, without a dissenting voice as far as I know, by Committee E of a conference in Washington, D.C., called by the United States Commissioner of Education to consider pressing problems confronting American schools in the years looming before us. The assignment of Committee E was to ascertain what long-range objectives should receive our attention between now and the all-too-rapidly approaching twenty-first century—a century that lies only as many years in the future as the year 1930 lies in the past.

As a member of Committee E, and one who helped to phrase the statement just read, I recall that its thirty-five or so members consisted of college and university presidents, several state commissioners of education, a variety of deans and other administrators, one or two superintendents of schools, and only three or four college and university professors. If I am right in my impression that educational administrators are not exactly noted for their radical views, and that the majority of Committee E's participants typified the higher echelons of educational leadership in America, then I hope you will agree that the quotation is extraordinary.

Not only does it affirm in unqualified terms the dominant values expressed in that wonderful credo of man's common dignity, the United Nations' Universal Declaration of Human Rights; it also ties together world civilization and education as copartners in behalf of those values. Not only does it recognize the individual as deserving of utmost fulfillment; it equally recognizes that individuals are social beings who attain fulfillment in maximum cooperation with and service to other social beings. Not only does the statement regard education as an enterprise dedicated to noble purposes, but it insists with comparable forthrightness that education is a "primary instrument," a powerful means, by which changes may be made so that these purposes can be achieved.

I will not trouble you with the more specific recommendations that Committee E developed in support of the quotation. What I do wish to underscore is that this statement could mark a turning point in the thinking of American education as a whole. We all know that for some years now the theory and practice of learning and teaching, of curriculum development, of support and control of education—indeed, of virtually every phase of education from the elementary school to the college and adult level—have been fraught with bickering, cross-purposes, and astonishing befuddlement. The recent pronouncement of the Educational Policies Commission, entitled "The Central Purpose of American Education," is only one of many illustrations that educational leaders are as often confused as clear-minded, as often eclectic or superficial as unified or consistent, as often prone to compromise for the sake of so-called harmony as to come to terms with the issues that confront education in our "time of trouble."

I borrow the phrase "time of trouble" from Arnold Toynbee, who, perhaps as ably as any diagnostician of contemporary history, has been calling our attention to the perilous period through which the world now stumbles. To review again the evidence for this assertion is surely unnecessary here. One need only note one among a great number of facts—the fact that the nuclear arsenals of both the United States and the Soviet Union already contain sufficient explosive power to destroy a large part of all life on the planet. Surely this one reality is enough in itself to demonstrate that mankind is indeed confronted with a "time of trouble" completely without precedent. The grim possibility exists that the year 2000 will never be recorded by a human hand because no human brain, the architect of human time, will be alive to herald that event.

It should not be asserted, of course, that all members of Committee E were equally disturbed by the crisis in which we are immersed. Since a characteristic American habit is to be optimistic and shortsighted even in the face of cataclysm, some members probably were much less disturbed than others were. I cannot believe, however, that a single member wished to evade the conclusion that the goals now demanded of education can no longer be expressed in traditional formulations.

A "time of trouble," however, is also a "time of opportunity"—opportunity to project fresh, bold objectives that can arouse our profession into concerted, adventurous, farsighted policies and programs. I choose so to interpret the intent of Committee E. In the spirit of its statement, I hold with the strongest conviction of which I am capable that our schools and colleges, abroad as well as in America, require one overarching purpose, by comparison with which all others are of subordinate importance. This purpose is to channel and release the full resources of education in behalf of the creation of a world civilization, one that is capable both of preventing destruction and of providing the peace and abundance that men everywhere crave.

The implications of world civilization

The remainder of this discussion is devoted to some of the major changes, opportunities, and problems that confront our profession when we take this purpose seriously, when we come to realize that polite platitudes are not enough if we are to translate the full implications of world civilization into the terms of a hardheaded, practical, and militant imperative.

But world civilization is anything but a simple purpose to delineate. This is understandable. The history of cultures has been for the most part ethnocentric history. People have viewed themselves and their world in the parochial perspective of their own biased frames of reference, their own limited institutional patterns of custom, practice, and value.

Nationalism, particularly, has been and still remains far more forceful in shaping men's loyalties than internationalism ever has. Even today, face to face with the most imminent danger of destruction that the human race has ever known, nationalism blinds and paralyzes the majority of us so that we are ready to go to any lengths, even to wholesale slaughter, in order to protect it. Countless millions of soldiers have been destroyed on the battlefields of history, as well as countless millions of children and other innocent victims, because of the hypnotic spell that national pride and hatred exert over reasoned judgment and conduct.

The path to fulfillment of the paramount new obligations of education is therefore strewn with obstacles. We must attack them without minimizing how stubborn they are. One important step forward is accordingly to provide constant, not just incidental, opportunity for young citizens to confront these obstacles. The issue of nationalism requires increasingly realistic, sophisticated treatment beginning as early as possible, certainly by the fourth or fifth grade.

This is only one urgent issue, however. Other kinds of human strife that narrow and distort a world perspective equally require treatment.

An example is the evil of racialism, which has achieved so much to alienate people of different pigmentations from one another, and to generate, even within a single nation such as our own, untold bitterness and violence. Almost if not equally pernicious have been the wars and persecutions fomented by the great religions, including Christianity, and the continued virulence of anti-Semitism and other forms of religious-cultural hostility. Nor, finally, can education ignore, except by deliberate evasion, the economic causes of national, racial, and even religious strife. The exploitation of natural resources, including the human, for the sake of pecuniary gain, and the power struggle for markets—these have nearly always functioned as necessary conditions of much of the sorry spectacle of history as perennial human conflict.

Although the countervailing requirement of education for world civilization is thus education in the hurdles that loom in the face of its accomplishment, diagnosis is only a portion of the task. Diagnosis demands prognosis. If citizens are to realize that they are, or certainly should be, engaged in the building of such a civilization, then two further problems arise. One, of course, is how to characterize world civilization so that it becomes a purpose glowing with significance—one that we come to embrace with at least the same intensity and passion that past and present cultures have taught us to feel toward a single nation or religion. The second problem is epitomized by the final words of Committee E's statement that "education is a primary instrument of social change and social welfare." On this basis, we should determine not merely the objective of world civilization, but also the strategies required to overcome the obstructions in its way, and to assure the constructions demanded for its attainment. Education has always been a reciprocity of ends and means, of purposes and processes, working together within a common human framework.

The meaning of world civilization: myth as symbol

Consider first the problem of meaning, the meaning of world

civilization. The key difficulty was anticipated long ago by the great philosopher, David Hume. "There is no such passion in human minds," he said, "as the love of mankind, merely as such." Hume was right: one can only love that which possesses clear imagery and definite tangibility. Yet we know that men do come to love whole communities, sometimes even large nations. How is this possible? The answer is that, through long centuries of experience, cultures have learned to transform the abstract into the concrete through vivid, stirring symbols, so that men can project and extend their immediate perceptions to more inclusive wholes. The vision of world civilization is, upon our shrinking planet of closer and closer involvement, probably much more open to this kind of symbolization than were any of the great world religions or empires of past history. Especially is this true when we recall the amazing new facilities for graphic, rapid communication never before available.

One of the richest of resources for the creation of a meaningful world civilization is, I believe, the idea of myth. Now I gladly admit that myth, as commonly understood, is uncongenial to educational thinking; it connotes all sorts of magical, irrational fantasies. I gladly admit, too, that myth often deserves these connotations, and to the extent that they remain relevant today they are properly suspect.

But as the Harvard psychiatrist Henry A. Murray indicates in the fascinating symposium *Myth and Mythmaking*, the import of the term myth is far more germane to modern experience than these conventional notions imply. Though myth is rooted primarily in ancient religion, as in Greece, we may note one or two of Murray's definitions. A "mythic representation," for example, is a sensuous, graphic "representation of an imagined situation or series of events, especially, today, a story or drama in poetic prose—not an abstract, conceptual (scientific) model of a certain class of events...." Another quote from Murray: Education's function is to present "an example of a better type of action..., or of the solution of a distressful conflict, or of a better way of life or better target of endeavor [which] educes emulative efforts and thereby changes personalities and/or their modes of living."

Murray points out, however, that in the face of the "probability" (note that he does not say "possibility") of "the mutual extermination of the technologically more advanced nations," in the face also of "the senescence of the traditional religions and their present incapacity...to bring forth the vision of a better world," he finds no "mythic patterns which are appropriate to the magnitude and the exigency of the confronting situation. To succeed...such mythic patterns will have to be as radical and revolutionary as the Sermon on the Mount."

One of the other symposium contributors, Mark Schorer, further sharpens the meaning of myth as it applies to our problem. It is, he says, "a large controlling image that gives philosophical meaning to the facts of ordinary life He quotes the anthropologist Bronislaw Malinowski as asserting that myth is "an indispensable ingredient of all culture."

In common with these scholars, I take the position that education today faces a thrilling, unique opportunity to enlist its energies in the effort to create a new myth for the emerging age—a myth that is, as Murray demands, "radical and revolutionary"; a myth impelled both by the ominous portents of disaster and the realizable hopes of a technological and cultural renascence; a myth that could contribute magnificently and eloquently to the emergence of a unified mankind that regards itself as a single whole, while yet respecting and encouraging variety and plurality within that single whole.

How, more specifically, may education undertake the task? In accordance with Murray's insistence that myths are never to be regarded as abstract, scientific models but rather as creative dramas, the first requirement in education is to press for reversal in the agenda of primary and secondary educational priorities. At present, as we all know, the natural sciences and mathematics take precedence. I do not deny that these fields are indispensable. I do deny that they are so essential as to force us to relegate the arts to a frequently feeble, innocuous position in most of our schools. The amount of money, the number of competent teachers of art, the quality of resources that the schools provide to enable learners to become painters, musicians, sculptors, actors, dancers, or poets are scandalously inadequate compared to provisions for almost any other area of learning. The consequence is that, for every promising young artist developed in our schools, we can count upon dozens if not hundreds of chemists, physicists, and engineers.

We all know, too, that the causes for this weighting of priorities lie in recent political developments. We do not, however, sufficiently consider whether this weighting, being the consequence of expediency and short-range objectives fostered by the fears and insecurities of an adroitly cultivated Cold War psychology, is anywhere nearly as defensible as the longer-range objectives that could result when we obtain a wider, more balanced perspective on the crisis of our time.

For, as Toynbee and other seekers of such a perspective have long been reminding us, the conflicts of the communist and capitalist spheres are only symptomatic of a vastly deeper malaise. Few well-informed experts now contend, for example, that the Soviet Union intends to attack the United States, any more than the United States intends to attack the Soviet Union; the governments of both nations know only too well that in our nuclear age both would be the victims. Equally, increasing numbers of experts recognize that economic, political, educational, cultural, and other differences between the two systems, although far from trivial, are in various respects diminishing rather than intensifying. Consider only the recent cultural exchanges among artists of both nations, or the comparable advances in space exploration. The more communication widens, as it gradually has been widening between both countries, the more similarities begin to appear and the greater the areas of interest shared by ordinary citizens.

These shared areas of interest, which grow everywhere that cultures have freedom to meet and intermingle, reinforce my contention that the single strongest need among human beings, whatever their race, creed, or nationality, is to find a common ground, a place on which to stand, not against one another, but with one another. But this common ground cannot be cultivated merely by technological advancement. It can be cultivated also, and far more tellingly, through the symbols of mythical communion. Such symbols proclaim the universality of human strivings and human hopes in the ways that music or drama or other creations of the esthetic man are able to proclaim them.

Here, then, is the reason why education in America, no less than in the Soviet Union or many other countries, has reversed the proper order of priorities. The natural sciences are not more important than the arts in the education required by our time. On the contrary, the arts, regarded now as the total enterprise of human creativity, are still more important. The achievement of world civilization is concomitant with its mythologizing. Its mythologizing is concomitant with millions of efforts, some simple, some prodigious, to capture the most intrinsic, poignant, and expressive experiences of human beings wherever they may be. These efforts range from the handsome ebony figure carved in the jungle by an African Bushman to the symphonies of Prokofiev and the poetry of Robert Frost; from the eager probings of an undiscovered young painter in a Burmese rural school to the breathtaking celebration of the cycle of man by Norway's majestic sculptor, Gustav Vigeland.

The mythologizing of world civilization is not, of course, achievable only through the free flow of esthetic communication. This is necessary, and the schools can help to advance it with a fullness and vibrancy that they have scarcely begun to provide. But even more imperative is, in Murray's words, "the vision of a better world" that is "appropriate to the magnitude and exigency of the confronting situation." Such a vision is, without a doubt, religious in quality. It is so, not in terms of historic doctrines or particular theologies, but in the sense that religious experience, whatever its special cultural form, is invariably the searching for and commitment to the widest, most significant whole that human beings are able to envisage.

The whole of such religious experience includes what Tillich calls man's "ultimate concern"—his ever-restless quest for the meaning of life and existence. The dawning age of space, with its ever-receding edges, beckons man to stretch further and further out from his own puny planet into the galactocentric universe. Thus it stirs man's imagination as never before to embrace wider and wider compasses of that universe. Indeed, it reinvigorates his primitive sense of awe and mystery, creating a mood radiant with wonderment, yet tempered by despair at the ultimate incomprehensibility of space and time.

The demand for a new myth of world civilization is not thereby diminished. If anything, man, perceiving himself in such a cosmic context, more easily perceives himself also as bound into a whole. You and I are something like the characters in Barrie's play, *The Admirable Crichton.* When shipwrecked on a lonely island in the midst of a vast ocean, they learned how trivial, how absurd, were their class and racial differences by contrast with their desperate need to survive and to cooperate.

The myth of a convergent mankind requires qualities of pathos, struggle, hope, and mutuality much like those illustrated in Barrie's play. The goal of a family of nations joining together in a guarantee of peace, in pervasive respect for one another's customs and unique qualities, in delight at opportunities to share with one another in enriching their divergent ways of life—here is the first goal that education should engender in the mind and the heart of every child and every adult.

Designs for world organization

But the goal of world civilization, however captivating as "mythic representation," also requires definitive designs in the form of political, economic, and social organization. Esthetic components, therefore, have to be related integrally with components from the social sciences. Education faces arduous tasks in bringing straight to the center of the curriculum a host of knotty problems in international government, in the development, distribution, and control of natural and industrial resources, and even in the new functions that institutions such as education itself should play in the future order.

Take, for example, the question of the kind of political structures that will have to be erected. Here the role of education, certainly in America, is to appraise every important alternative proposal for international organization, totalitarian and democratic alike, and to weigh these proposals objectively, encouraging learners to dissent frankly whenever they wish, but at the same time taking a firm stand for educational policy based on democratic political principles. Such principles would imply a world organization in which determination of every comprehensive policy embracing the welfare of human beings everywhere on earth is, first, finally authorized by the largest possible majority, and, second, perpetually subject to review and revision through the instrumentality of public criticism on the part of any minority that disapproves of a given policy.

No one denies that the operation of democracy on a global scale will be complex in the extreme. Even on a small scale it is complex enough. We have no alternative, however, but to try to make democracy operate effectively on every level, small and large. Study of such designs for international order as those of the World Federalists deserve scrupulous attention by all young citizens in the public schools.

Equally difficult is the question of international authority. As we know only too well from the sad history of the League of Nations, and now from the precarious status of the United Nations, national rivalries can undermine any world organization. Indeed, they will almost surely do so unless the power of the whole is unequivocally greater than the power of any one of its parts. Exactly as in the case of our own union of many states, federal authority backed by power to enforce its mandates is accordingly indispensable to democratic world government. The *ad hoc* armed forces established by the United Nations to deal with disturbances in Lebanon and the Congo prove, however, that international power exercised to prevent war and to restore order is already workable. Moreover, public opinion polls reveal that large majorities of citizens favor such forces. The crucial issue, then, must be faced squarely by learners in the schools. It must be faced, not by evasion, not by compromise, not by opportunistic schemes to have our international cake and eat it too, but with the realization that sovereignty as we have known it in history is completely outmoded, insidiously deceptive, and utterly dangerous. The United States, no less than any nation, will have to abrogate its traditional sovereignty with regard to all policies effecting the maintenance of world order and prosperity in favor of the one available alternative—international sovereignty. When and only when this issue is faced and resolved will you and I no longer pay verbal tribute to world civilization while still intending in our hearts to preserve the status quo. Still more crucially, we will not be asking our students to engage in such a hypocrisy.

We all recognize that Pennsylvania is not a sovereign state with regard to policies directed at the welfare and interest of the federal union, and that the citizens of Pennsylvania with almost no exceptions accept this principle at the same time that they properly wish to preserve their authority over policies limited to state welfare and interest. It becomes essential for us now to take another giant step forward in the evolution of political relations. This step is world government. Such a government would have to profit, to be sure, by the rugged experience of the United Nations in attempting to maintain order, but in it supreme coercive power would be as much greater in its enforceability over individual nations as federal power in our country is indisputably and legitimately greater than that of any single one of our fifty states.

But even such a government, however imperative, is not enough. A further characteristic of world civilization that the supreme purpose of education must confront is economic in base. No social order, small or large, can hope to be democratic except in name as long as control of natural resources (land, oil, water, minerals, air) remains in the hands of minorities. Trite as the statement may sound, political and economic democracy is a completely reciprocal objective. It applies just as fully to world civilization as it does to a coal mining town in West Virginia or to a diamond mining village in South Africa.

The schools and colleges of our country are therefore as derelict in their duties when they skirt or underplay problems of economic power as they are when they avoid or superficialize an issue like sovereignty. One such problem is the nature and extent of imperialism, as manifested in the more blunt practices of, for example, the older British and Dutch Empires, or in the more polite and more surreptitious practices of the Shell Oil Company in the Near East or the American Fruit Company in Latin America.

Economic exploitation and deprivation are, indeed, so chronic in the world today that education could render no worse disservice than to lead young people into assuming that the affluent society in which we live is typical of other societies. So long as some seventy percent of the earth's population remains undernourished, no better commentary upon American provincialism could easily be chosen than indifference to or ignorance of this appalling truth. World civilization means, therefore, that industrialization of underdeveloped areas can be morally justified only when stringent safeguards are set up against exploitation of human labor as well as of the riches of mineral or soil. It means that consumer cooperatives and other forms of democratic economic participation should he extended systematically and internationally by a World Economic Authority. Such an authority requires power duly delegated by the organization of nations to promote grassroots programs of agricultural and industrial development aimed at nothing short of a global standard of living comparable to that of the United States.

As we push toward this perfectly attainable economic goal for peoples of all races and nationalities, still further problems will arise that require attention through education. One, certainly, is population planning. I need not remind you that even the United States will soon jeopardize its standard of living at the present rate of population increase. It is likely that at least twice as many people as now live upon it will be thronging our planet by the year 2000—that is, about six billions. Here again education for world civilization means confrontation of inescapable issues, in this case birth control. Unless we in education are willing to sidestep such issues because we are intimidated by provincial sensitivities, we have no choice but to guarantee forth-right study of every problem—political economic, social, moral. The most reprehensible error we could make, if I grasp the full intent of the quotation from Committee E, would be, on the one hand, to address ourselves to the purposes of world civilization, but then, on the other hand, to censor or otherwise delimit full educational analysis and interpretation of its implications. Problems of international sovereignty, worldwide economic planning, and systematic, internationally sponsored population control exemplify my meaning.

Nevertheless, a great deal more than I have been able to select for illustration would have to be included in any comprehensive characterization. The need, for example, of a World Education Authority comparable in resources and influence to a World Economic Authority, is one further illustration. Its beginnings are already discernible in the valiant efforts of UNESCO to tackle illiteracy and a hundred other cultural problems despite disgracefully meager funds. Again, although I have chosen to place esthetic qualities highest on the list of means for the dramatization of world civilization, I surely do not intend to relegate the biological, physical, and behavioral sciences to a trivial place. Of course, any plausible conception of world order makes generous room for both pure and applied scientific research and advancement, which many authorities predict will proceed during the next quarter century at an even more accelerated pace than in the quarter century immediately past. Actually, science and art, rightly understood, are not antithetical: both afford boundless opportunity for human creativity.

The path toward world civilization

It is necessary to deal more briefly with our final major question: the means required to attain the end. In some respects, of course, I have already been discussing means. When teachers become deeply enough committed to the goal of world civilization, its mythologizing begins in kindergarten and continues all the way through college and far into adult life. A wide range of social and other scientific studies equally contribute toward the overarching goal, even when they may not always directly or obviously do so. In many instances, a particular course of study, say mathematics, may seem to have no relation to the goal at all. Yet I would insist that, once the great transcending purpose is sufliciently infused through the whole fabric of education and through the personnel who perform its work, no single facet of the curriculum, no single skill or subject, no extracurricular activity, no administrative task, can or should ever be completely severed from that transcending purpose. Or, to restate an earlier contention, all education will become pervaded with a universally religious quality.

The concern of Committee E with education as means—that is, as an instrument of social change—is far from adequately answered by these generalizations. I wish in addition to make it plain that when education is audaciously enough conceived, it becomes at least as powerful an agency of cultural transformation toward world civilization as do the more familiar agencies of social change, such as politics. For much too long a time, we have failed to understand that education's role in history has never been merely one of transmission of customs or of other cultural patterns; it has often been just as pervasively one of modification and innovation.

With rapid emergence of the behavioral sciences, we are beginning to discover a great deal about the dynamics of change, including democratically planned change. Hitherto in history, change has occurred largely by accident of strife. Therefore I reiterate that teachers, the professional bloodstream of education, now require training in all of the behavioral sciences from psychiatry to anthropology. In fact, thorough training in them should become the core of their preparation, just as the biological sciences are the core of preparation for the medical profession. At the same time, teachers, thus equipped far more competently to undertake both the galvanization of education for the purpose of world civilization, and the activization of education as cultural change in the direction of that purpose, should assume chief responsibility for the means and ends of education. They should refuse to relinquish that responsibility to anyone else.

Meanwhile, one of the steps that the profession could take, even during the slow process of its own badly needed strengthening as an independently organized profession, is in the form of vigorous support for pilot projects within present day curriculums—projects pointing toward world civilization as their unifying theme. Beginnings are already scattered through the schools and colleges in courses dealing with international relations or the United Nations. Nevertheless, such projects are altogether too rare even on the college level. A national survey conducted by the Carnegie Corporation discovered that understanding of international affairs by American students "is more provincial than in any comparable country"; that seniors graduate from college "with little more knowledge about foreign affairs than they had as freshmen"; and that isolationist attitudes are chronic on all college levels.

The time is long overdue, therefore, when we of the teaching profession should ourselves take the lead in correcting this shocking imbalance. One way to do so is to launch experimental curriculum designs, especially on the secondary level. In urging that world civilization serve as the central concept of integration, I do not suggest that conventional subjects such as foreign languages or history be omitted; I do contend that first things need to come first, and that if one or another sterile subject goes by the boards in order to make room for the cutting-edge analyses and interpretations for which I am pleading, then let it go by the boards. The important point is that world civilization, embracing as it does, directly or indirectly, every significant aspect of human life and destiny, provides a way to harmonize the general education of young citizens that is comparable in vitality to no other way.

Such an innovation through pilot curriculum designs would be, in its academic standards, anything but easy. On the contrary, it ought to be much tougher than most of what passes for secondary education today. But it could and should prove to be exciting education, and exciting education rarely needs to worry about lack of motivation, poor discipline, or sloppy scholarship. Remember, too, that the kind of experimental designs I am envisaging are anything but the eggcrate structures of discrete pieces and cubicles of subject matter so typical of the American high school today. On the contrary, the required design is an esthetic unity, permeated throughout with the dramatic qualities of "mythic representation." Much more could be suggested as to the nature of the educational processes by which we should struggle to reach that paramount goal. Regretfully, I have been able to offer little more than a sketch of the adventure that awaits education in our "time of trouble." I would leave no ambiguity, however, as to my theme.

The entire purpose and process of education should be reconstructed. Man lives in a period fraught with the greatest peril he has ever encountered. Simultaneously, he lives in a period of such awesome discovery and scientific advance that he is capable of producing a way of life far more abundant and humanly creative than any he has hitherto imagined. In such a period, timeworn curriculums, traditional teaching and learning practices, indeed much of the inherited structure and function of education, become outmoded. Education, more than any other institution created by the only culture-building animal on earth, has the responsibility and opportunity to bring to all the children and adults of all countries the full import of the fearful and promising age in which we live. Shortsightedness, caution, timidity, grubbing imagination, confusions in theory—these are obstacles that can and should be broken through by teachers and students who hunger for inspiration and confidence in the vast potential power of education. There are tens of millions of such teachers and students. All they ask is the chance to respond to magnetic goals and concerted programs of democratic action. The worst failure that educational leaders could commit today would be that of denying these millions the privilege of demonstrating their eagerness to transform education into an unconquerable agency of cultural change—change directed toward the single most compelling goal of our age: world civilization.

Appendix

A Charter for Educational Leadership

A charter for educational leadership adequate to our age can only be constructed within a great conception of education itself.

This generalization applies, however, to widely differing conceptions, all the way from Plato and Aristotle to Comenius, Pestalozzi, and Dewey. Nor is it limited to philosophers invariably treated in the history textbooks. A case could be made, I believe, to the effect that theories less orthodox or familiar to American students of education—the Marxist, Confucianist, Existentialist, and Zen Buddhist are a good sample—all promulgate educational outlooks in their respective ways that stretch man's imagination and push his horizons far beyond his conventional self.

Accordingly, rather than to make a case for one or another of the major approaches to the question before us, I prefer to elicit the aid of eight guiding concepts—concepts not necessarily identified with any one of the great philosophies of education, yet surely reflecting the considerable influence of several. I shall call them: creativity, audacity, directiveness, convergence, commitment, confrontation, involvement, and control.

I do not suggest that they exhaust the range of useful concepts;

more might be added and two or three might be condensed to reduce the number. Certainly they overlap. Nevertheless, they serve to lift the sights of the educational leader and to help him move toward a clear expression of his own philosophy of education.

I. Creativity

I begin with *creativity* for a trio of reasons. First, it is one of the most neglected and least understood concepts of all contemporary education. Second, it at once intimates that the needed new approach to educational leadership departs radically from traditional approaches. Consequently, third, in helping to reshape the image of the educational leader it restores to him some of the personal qualities (originality is one) which never should have been weakened in the first place.

As long as the schools and colleges of America continue to yield to industrial, governmental, and military pressures and therefore to give priority to the physical sciences, mathematics, and other quantitative disciplines at the expense of the arts and other qualitative disciplines, just so long do they contribute to a standard for the educated man that distorts, narrows, prostrates, and eventually sickens whole populations of young learners. The relatively trivial amount of time, money, and competent direction provided in the majority of American schools for intensive, sustained involvement in the great arts of man—compared, that is, with the time, money, and competent direction provided for the physical sciences and other allies of our technology-oriented culture—is a current educational scandal. To the degree that leaders of our schools condone or at least quietly acquiesce in this imbalance, they must take responsibility for its prolongation.

If, however, they are willing to resist the pressures of our power elites, if they are alert to the dangers in such pressures, and if they are prepared to challenge the apologists for current educational opportunism who speak and write so influentially today, these leaders must look unto themselves. In order to appreciate and support the creative functions of education, they will have to demonstrate their own capacity for creativity—a capacity to which I very much fear the conventional preparation afforded by most college departments of school administration is anything but conducive.

Let me pinpoint the kind of orientation that would help to correct this imbalance. I am thinking here of an important posthumous work by Harold Rugg. Titling his book simply *Imagination*, Professor Rugg summarized more than a decade of exhaustive research directed toward the goal of how education might itself become energized by the *élan* of creativity. It was his conviction that vast though largely untapped resources are available both from the biological, psychological, and social sciences, and from the philosophies of the Orient at least as much as from the Occident, which now enable us to grasp the meaning of the creative act. One of his chief hypotheses, largely confirmed in the book, was that the full significance of the creative act can never be delineated in terms of the canons of conventional psychology. For this reason he gave special attention to what he called "The Theorem of the Transliminal Mind," an "antechamber" between consciousness and unconsciousness where the actual experience of creative insight explodes into significance.

What, more directly, is the relevance of the first concept for our focal concern? The creative leader is one who, having been made aware not only of the key meanings of this concept but of his own obligations to them, tries his best to carry the following applications into daily operation:

He encourages his faculty to deviate from curriculum structures or teaching regularities, to try out provocative ideas, and to make mistakes without fear of recrimination in the attempt to carry them out.

He exerts continuous effort to place all of the arts, from painting and music to poetry and the dance, on an equal level of time, money, and competence with the sciences and their allied disciplines in the total program.

He encourages students with any kind of creative flair to let themselves go in their own distinctive ways. Precocious talents may not, of course, always fall within the fields of art. Some will certainly appear in science—fashioning a piece of apparatus to be tested in a biochemistry experiment, for example. But the point is that the learner who reveals originality in any direction whatsoever should be afforded maximum leeway, regardless of schedules and requirements, to nourish and release it.

Lastly, the educational leader himself becomes to his faculty and students a kind of symbol of creative education. He, too, proposes new approaches to old structures, deviates from routines, and regards the school as one place where adults as well as children are invited to seek outlets for their own urge to express unique interests and capacities.

The routine-conditioned leader, the conforming and cautious leader, will promote and sanction the kind of education that mirrors his own qualities of personality. By the same token the imaginative leader, the courageous and adventurous leader, will promote the kind of education that encourages his qualities. Creativity, in short, becomes one important gauge of his own right to leadership at all.

II. Audacity

The interrelations of our cluster of concepts become evident at once when we turn to the second: *audacity*. Indeed, the first measure of leadership of which I have just spoken surely requires one to be bold and daring. The two concepts are not synonymous, however. Particularly is it true that some individuals may show audacity—politicians, for example—and yet be characterized by nothing more than presumptuousness or brazen ambition.

Among the qualities of audacity which I wish to highlight, the most crucial in my view is vision. The leader must be capable of envisioning the role that education plays in shaping the future of humanity, and thus of picturing as graphically as possible the kind of civilization that we are now capable of constructing upon earth. In common therefore with followers of one of the great traditions in speculative thought, I am suggesting that education should provide generous room for cultivating the utopian mood. The term utopian here is used, not to suggest an escape from reality, but rather to suggest such penetrating projections in the history of thought as Plato's, More's, Bacon's, and Bellamy's, and in our own day the clairvoyant designs of the foremost utopian thinker in America, Lewis Mumford.

Education thus conceived is by no means, then concerned merely with the past experiences of mankind nor even with its present ones. The stress of the typical curriculum upon these two dimensions of time to the neglect of the third dimension is one of the reasons why young people so often seem blasé about either the dangers or promises of the impending decades—dangers and promises for which they must, nevertheless, take responsibility.

At least one way to correct this deficiency is to provide a substantial place in learning, beginning in the very early years and extending all the way through the college years, for increasingly sophisticated attention to resources already available to man for rebuilding his major institutions. The lightning-like transformations of recent years that have resulted from our scientific revolutions, and now the arrival of the first age of space in history—these events surely provide a marvelous opportunity for explorations of the future of humanity. The popularity of science fiction testifies to student readiness for high motivation.

Thus another way that the educational leader evokes the quality of creative experience already noted under the first concept is in his support of audacious visions of the future as an imperative educational experience. At least one further quality is, however, necessary to the amalgam of our second concept. This is open-mindedness. As I regard it, the utopian mood never aims at ultimate perfection. Such an aim only invites rigid-minded faith in some form of spurious salvation either in heaven or on earth. I see no contradiction between the requirement of far-reaching cultural portrayals based upon substantial knowledge of all of the sciences and the arts, and the equal requirement of adequate room for radical corrections or additions to these portrayals.

Return now to some practical implications of our second concept. The audacious school leader is like an audacious architect. Not only is he willing to break from traditional designs in the manner of a Frank Lloyd Wright; he is daring enough to test out designs that have not thus far even been attempted. Furthermore, he thinks of education not in terms of one-year plans or even five-year plans but thirty-five-year plans. He realizes that the community—local, regional, national, and international—is bound to be very different a mere thirty-five years hence (when the year 2000 arrives). In budget planning, therefore, he constantly reminds himself and his constituency that the total of eighteen or so billions now spent on education in America are but a fraction of what we shall need if education is to keep pace with other sweeping innovations already well under way.

Nor does he confine his vision to America. He knows that a World Education Authority is necessary, one with international funds and international power sufficient to wipe out illiteracy everywhere on earth and to provide fine teachers and equip them so that every child, not only at home but in Africa, South America, or Asia, may develop his powers to the maximum. He knows that only such an audacious policy will do in the closely knit world of the near tomorrow.

III. Directiveness

Directiveness, our third concept, is like the second in the sense that it both extends earlier concepts and anticipates those to follow. The creative and audacious projections demanded of education also require a course of development with purpose. It is not enough to look well into the future, necessary though this requirement is. It is also essential to recognize that the course of man's evolution depends entirely upon his own organized abilities to direct that course. Education in this sense is a prime agency of cultural change. It is not, as some educators would have us suppose, an agency that performs its chief duties when it reflects and transmits the movements of other institutions. It does perform a necessary transmitting function, certainly. But it likewise performs, as the testimony of anthropology and cultural history demonstrates, a modifying and reconstructive function. Education follows but it also leads.

The concept of directiveness is especially helpful, then, when it views education as a continuity of processes and goals. Without substantive goals there can be no real direction for the energies of the school. Without processes there can be no hope of progress toward such impelling goals as I have just discussed.

To deepen this idea a little further, we may return for a moment to the significance of evolution. As numerous authorities have pointed out, evolution occurs in three great stages: the preorganic stage of nonliving matter, the concern of sciences like astronomy and geology; the organic stage, the concern of the biological sciences; and the postorganic stage, the concern of the sciences of human behavior. Now the extraordinary fact about the postorganic stage is that it is the only one of the three not entirely the result of blind forces in nature. Only it, in other words, contains within it the power of conscious awareness with which man, alone among earthly species, is endowed. Through it he remembers the mistakes he has made in the past and imagines ways in which to prevent them in the future. Man alone, in short, is the evolution-directing animal.

This does not suggest that man can ever be positive that the direction he pursues is the best of all possible directions. Sir Julian Huxley has indicated that evolutionary change as a natural process is characterized by three crucial features: irreversibility, novelty, and variety. Like the levels of preorganic and organic evolution, the postorganic level never repeats itself; always one discovers a proliferation of forms of human experience that are unique and diverse. Chance plays a role in the midst of order.

An educational leader who is directive may thus be defined in one sense as a leader concerned to gear the powers of his institution to evolutionary processes on the postorganic level. Abstract as this statement surely must sound, it is not at all abstract in the mandate that follows from it: to conceive of education as the foremost means by which man learns how to shoulder the momentous tasks which the mutations of organic nature have thrust upon his species. Not only does evolution tell us that purposes are man-generated and that we alone, whether we like it or not, must determine what we want these purposes to be; it tells us too that the processes by which we struggle to achieve them lie entirely in our collective hands.

As Hermann J. Muller, the great Nobel prize winner in genetics, has insisted, the theory of evolution thus supports a remarkable opportunity to unify the whole curriculum of general education. It brings the physical, biological, and human sciences, as well as the arts, into meaningful integration. More than this, it provides education with a graphic sense of its own indispensable importance to the survival and development of man. The educational leader who grasps the full intent of what Muller and Huxley are implying becomes not only a directive leader but a senior partner in the full evolutionary enterprise of nature.

IV. Convergence

In turning to *convergence* as the fourth idea in our cluster, I am chiefly concerned to underscore another aspect of Huxley's conception: increase of organization. Evolution is, one might contend, a dialectical process. At the same time that it produces increasing diversity, it also produces increasing unity. The remarkable paleontologist and philosopher, Teilhard de Chardin, has helped us, more profoundly perhaps than any other recent scholar, to understand this polaristic law. Although blurred by theological predilections, de Chardin's writings nevertheless sparkle with insights into the convergent nature of cosmic and human evolution.

Let me quote just one of his statements: "The most conspicuous human characteristic," says de Chardin, "is the fantastic and unquestionable property exhibited by mankind of not only continuing to diverge and differentiate as many other animal groups but, in addition, to become more and more irresistibly united into a single natural whole. The...specific characteristic of the modern world is no longer divergency but acceleration of a process forcing man to become economically, and mentally one...[Man] is forced biologically to be one—or to fail."

The implications of such convergence for the task of education must be disturbing indeed to any leader in education not infected by complacency or cultural myopia. Not only does it suggest that blockages and resistances to interracial and other intergroup cooperation are contrary to the irreversible trends of evolutionary processes, it suggests equally that national, religious, and ethnic barriers violate these trends on a planetary scale. This is not to say, and de Chardin does not say it, that conflict is unnatural or that divergence is not also an essential phenomenon of man. Nevertheless, any kind of education that stands aloof from the convergent forces of postorganic evolution, or that seeks deliberately to obstruct them by policies of divisiveness or by a curriculum that avoids or distorts the compulsions of our age toward international order, is an education that deserves the indictment not only of any humanistic ethics but of the sciences of man.

And yet by such a standard, how can we in education honestly contend that our field is safe from this kind of indictment? More bluntly, how far is it true that school leaders in the North as well as in the South have militantly fought to eliminate de facto if not official segregation of children of Negro, Puerto Rican, or Mexican parentage or other children belonging to minority groups? How far have they been concerned with the more surreptitious segregations that result from economic stratifications of class and status, the religious segregations induced by the parochial school system, the isolation of millions of aged citizens from community involvement, or the uncomfortable discriminations against women exemplified by their almost total absence from national conferences of professors of school administration? Above all, how deeply have leaders in education been troubled over the persistent ideology of American superiority in the conflict of nations, or of the pressures to place allegiance to our nation over allegiance to a community of nations? The norm of convergence, when such questions are asked, points to a range of too largely ignored and certainly unfinished educational tasks.

If, however, convergence begins at home then it begins also in the organization of the schools themselves. And here still further tasks at once suggest themselves. One task to which I return under the concept of control, is that of providing for much wider cooperation than is now characteristic between faculty, students, parents, and administrators in the conduct of every institution concerned with education. Another task is that of reexamining and updating the whole tradition of local and state autonomy in the affairs of education. This tradition, in its sphere of influence, is becoming as inimical to convergent evolution as the segregation of races is inimical in its sphere. Still another task recalls my earlier plea for an audacious approach to education on nothing less than a world scale. Any convergence of nations requires a convergent role by education also—a goal possible only when and as a World Education Authority is organized and supported with many more times the funds and strength we now provide to that admirable vanguard of de Chardin's principle: the United Nations Educational Scientific and Cultural Organization.

V. Commitment

Commitment, the fifth concept, has been struggling for recognition long before now. The entire spirit of educational leadership which I am seeking to articulate is permeated with commitment. It is charged with basic convictions about the compulsions of a time of fearful dangers to the very survival of mankind, yet simultaneously with profound and passionate hope that mankind possesses more than enough good sense and competence to prevent the most ultimate of horrors.

Nevertheless, the notion that education in its public as well as private forms should develop commitment to goals that are something more than platitudes, that expect you and me to take sides rather than to remain supposedly neutral toward the urgent questions of our half-century—such a notion is still far from congenial to even a fair number of my fellow educational philosophers. Methodological preoccupations are invariably easier to justify than normative and substantive convictions. In less polite language, it is always safer to pretend or even seriously to attempt to be objective than it is to take a firm stand on any issue against which someone is bound to protest. We are familiar with the strategies through which noncommitment to anything except alleged objectivity is made to appear virtuous. One of these, of course, is to assert that a teacher or professor who does happen to care strongly enough to express vigorous commitments has fallen victim to some form of wild extremism or fanatical dogmatism.

Something of this strategy is employed by Professors S.T. Kimball and J.E. McClellan in defending their book, *Education and the New America*, perhaps the single most alarming work to come from the generation of younger educational theorists who have followed the period of Dewey orthodoxy. Thus, in responding to my own review, published in *The Harvard Educational Review*, McClellan skirts my criticisms of the book by the *ad hominem* device of repeatedly calling me "angry." But he adds a revealing comment: "I rather think that Mr. Brameld worships the Golden Calf of a 'democratic world community,' mistaking it for God.... We've offended his religion, for we don't advocate an education built around the worship of his (or any other) god. The attitude of critical disciplined intelligence and the attitude of emotional involvement are antithetical."

Please note three implications in these sentences. First, to reveal commitment to a democratic world community is to worship a "Golden Calf" and is therefore tantamount to a false commitment. Second, such commitment is to a false new "god," a new "religion." And third, it is antithetical to "disciplined intelligence" because it encourages "emotional involvement."

I emphatically reject all three implications in Professor McClellan's own meaning. I do not believe that commitment to a community of nations, based as it is upon the principle of evolutionary convergence, is a false commitment. The term "Golden Calf" is, in sober fact, insulting to millions of ordinary citizens in America and other countries, not to mention such committed philosophers as Bertrand Russell, who are working day and night for the peaceful world that is possible only through such a community of nations.

Nor do I believe that it is at all improper for education to be imbued with the quality of religiosity—certainly not if one defines that term in such nonsectarian terms as the total devotion of any person to the search for life's highest values. What is improper, of course, is any kind of education that allows religiosity to overcome the completely equal requirement of critical and constant readiness to examine every commitment and to correct every weakness that such examination may expose.

Finally and consequently, I do not believe that disciplined intelligence and emotional involvement are necessarily "antithetical" at all. Of course, it is possible for them to be antithetical. A major obligation of education as commitment, however, is to insure that rationality and emotionality are reciprocal experiences in the life of cultures, just as they can and indeed must become so in the life of any healthy, mature individual. The bifurcations that Professors McClellan and Kimball advocate are nothing less than a retreat from the moral obligations of contemporary education—and this at precisely the moment in human history when just such obligations and commitments to the convergent goals of mankind should be pivotal to education.

VI. Confrontation

The five concepts which I have thus far tried to delineate are, in one perspective, the chief substantive ends with which educational leadership should now concern itself. Of these, commitment to the end of an enforceable world order is by far the most compelling. It is the principal galvanizing concept of the five we have considered.

The three remaining concepts in our constellation are, by comparison, modal concepts—that is, they are ways by which the desirable goals of education and culture may crystallize into concrete achievement. Let us not, however, commit the error of separating one group of concepts sharply from the other. Each sort requires the other; neither by itself is sufficient.

The sixth concept, *confrontation*, suggests to the educational leader that audacious ends without tough-minded means are likely to become the wishful and tender-minded indulgences of well-intentioned people who never face the obstructions that block every step of their way. I readily admit that the school administrator who asks us to be realistic, to show common sense in realizing what he is up against as he faces and tries to mollify the pressure groups of his community, has my heartfelt sympathy. I do not envy him. No doubt it is much easier to be an educational philosopher!

And yet one wonders sometimes whether the indubitable fact of obstacles does not provide the perfect alibi for taking the easy way out, for making excuses that diminish the role of education to the unadventurous, timid, pedestrian policies and programs that continue to grip the majority of American schools of this generation. I would prefer, myself, to view obstacles in another way, to see them as placing upon education a much heavier rather than a lighter responsibility to meet them squarely, to assess their stubbornness, and to devise strategies sufficiently aggressive and goal-directed to attack and overcome them.

Two pervasive types of obstacles confront educators unwilling to settle for any easier alternative. One is subjective, the other objective, but both are inextricably related. By subjective obstacles, I mean those rooted in human nature itself, obstacles which the sciences of the human psyche have only begun to raise to the surface of understanding, much less to control. No informed person any longer denies the existence or the force of these unrational drives. And yet the scant attention still paid by most colleges of education to the prodigious impact of Sigmund Freud's contributions, or to neo-Freudian approaches such as Harry Stack Sullivan's, or even to anti-Freudian approaches such as that of Carl Rogers, is little less than a disgrace. Granting that psychiatric knowledge and practice are not wholly ignored by professional programs, the record is clear that neither are they stressed.

The preparation of *all* personnel intending to serve the schools and colleges, whether they are geometry teachers, guidance counselors, or school superintendents, calls for revamping of the entire program of educational psychology to include intensive and prolonged attention to the subjective spheres of human experience. Nor is the purpose of such a needed revamping chiefly academic. It is the hard-headed purpose of direct confrontation—confrontation with the realities of human conflict, hostility, anxiety, frustration, repression, and a whole range of other blockages to the release of man's creative powers.

Objective blockages are, in various ways, the reverse of the same coin. Some of these have been intimated in earlier remarks about resistances to convergence, segregation of minority groups being but one grim example. I need hardly emphasize that personality conflicts and their efflorescences of neurosis and psychosis are only too often much more the effect than the cause of social, economic, religious, and other conflicts in the wider culture.

The truth is that most colleges of education fail to provide prospective teachers with understanding of such psychocultural conflicts. It is even more dismally true that a majority of professional programs fail to provide competent or intensive work in anthropology, political psychology, or most other sciences of the social man. Large numbers of practicing teachers are almost totally ignorant of such giants of the social sciences as Karl Marx, Max Weber, Karl Mannheim, Thorstein Veblen, and Alfred L. Kroeber. Yet all of these men, plus a host of others, contribute beyond measure to interpreting and attacking the formidable obstacles that loom in the path of man's heroic struggles to fulfill his own expectations.

The confronting leader in education is one equipped with as much evidence of obstacles, and I underscore evidence of obstacles, as he is able to command. As a kind of physician of the ailments besetting human relationships, he knows that sound prognosis depends upon thorough, exacting diagnosis. The evidence of the best students of subjective and objective human behavior is not, therefore, acquired merely as understanding. It is evidence to be used clinically—in the classroom, in the neighborhood, on the playground, and above all in the work of the school as a laboratory of social innovation.

True enough, education today rarely provides this kind of laboratory. The fault, however, is not inherent in education. The fault is correctible. But it is correctible neither by the superficial and eclectic remedies of a widely heralded book called *The Education of American Teachers* nor by the anti-educationist contortions of *The Miseducation of American Teachers*. Only an audacious policy that places preparation for any kind of educational service on a level at least equal in standards to that of the medical profession will serve us now.

VII. Involvement

Of all the concepts that I have selected for consideration *involvement*, the seventh in our series, is perhaps most readily conceded. This concept has also been anticipated several times—in considering, for example, the need to bring the behavioral sciences of man and culture to bear upon real educational issues in real communities. Several further observations, however, are pertinent.

In the first place, involvement through education needs to utilize the still fairly new applied sciences of planned social change. I say "fairly new." It is true that intermittent attention has been paid for a long time to the strategies of action involved in, say, dissident political movements. Yet, it is also true that systematic research of the kind conducted by Ronald Lippitt into the climates of resilience and nonresilience to community change is still on the cutting edge of behavioral science. Particularly is there need for action research into the subcultures of schools as these relate to the planning operations of government, industry, labor, or other phases of cultural order. The educational leader who wishes his school to be a party to these operations needs to employ a variety of experts in the social sciences. At the same time, these experts will often find the school a fertile if neglected laboratory awaiting their own experimental ventures in planned social change.

In the second place, and in a somewhat different context, the whole nature of power in modern society requires fresh examination. The thesis of C. Wright Mills that power today is vested mainly in three elites—the political, industrial, and military—is a very unnerving one. It cannot be avoided by any leader willing to take seriously the preceding concept of confrontation. Particularly is it disturbing to those who still cherish faith in the capacity of public education to affect the direction of human evolution.

The involved leader in education will not gloss over the biting diagnoses of scholars such as Mills. Through them, however, he will come to realize that the profession of education, if it is ever to be powerful, will have to learn one lesson from other groups that are already powerful indeed. This is the lesson of collective strength, of the organized will that compounds the individual will in geometric ratio to the numbers of participants. Or, again in more everyday language, the educational profession has to learn to unite powerfully in support of its own rights and its own responsibilities.

Here I venture to state another guiding principle. The power elite that is potential also in the educational profession should not center in its administrative echelons. Necessary as administrative services certainly are, education as a profession consists primarily and properly of teachers. Accordingly, in my view, administrators should never be the rulers of teachers. Rather, teachers should be the rulers of administrators. I shall try to clarify this principle when I turn in a moment to the concept of educational control. My contention meanwhile is, I hope, unequivocal: we teachers should become strongly and independently organized for the good of our profession and service to the people. We are organized in neither way today. The involved leader, governed by the kind of philosophy of education toward which I am pointing, will support without hesitation this kind of power struggle for a free association or union of teachers not only within our nation but across many nations.

In the third place and on a less controversial point, the leader in education will encourage every member of his staff to try out unconventional proposals. The connection of this imperative with creativity has already been sufficiently stressed so that I need add only a single comment. Involvement in the form of educational breakthroughs should rarely occur on a wholesale basis. At first they must be tested as carefully prepared and relatively small-scale ventures. Only then, if they succeed, can they be extended to whole communities or even to whole nations. The pilot-project approach is familiar to all of us. But the strategy of educational involvement has hardly begun to make the most of this approach in widespread, experimental practice.

VIII. Control

And so we reach *control*, the eighth and final concept. It could, I think, be argued that here is the supreme integrating concept of educational leadership. And yet, is not control still another abstraction that can be interpreted in conflicting ways? Surely some kinds of control are highly immoral, others are relatively amoral, while still others are very moral indeed. The meaning of this concept is not to be found accordingly in its instrumental role alone—efficiency, most notably. A dictator can be efficient in the employment of the secret police, yet most of us hardly approve his actions. The real issue, of course, is that of moral or immoral ends, of the good or bad purposes that methods of control enhance.

And now for the first time in this discussion I must introduce the value-laden end: democracy. All of us in education become more than a little tired of this term, especially when we so often hear it uttered by convention speakers and professional hacks. Even so, I offer no apologies for regarding democracy as the capstone of our charter.

The truth is that the ideal of democracy, properly conceived, is still the most utopian, the most radical, and on a world scale the least realized of all the great political ideals thus far available to mankind.

The achievement of democracy means that the human race has finally grown up enough to take complete charge of its own affairs. On how much of the earth is this true? The achievement of democracy means that men no longer look to some absolute authority beyond themselves for guidance and direction. On how much of the earth is this true? The achievement of democracy means that children and adults of all races, religions, and nationalities are the possessors, directors, and consumers of the resources of land, machines, the sciences, and the arts. On how much of the earth is this true? Finally, the achievement of democracy means that education from nursery school through the university is open and completely free to all learners everywhere, for as long as they can benefit by education. On how much of the earth is this true?

The definition of control which I submit to you relates immediately to this thoroughly and radically democratic goal. It is based on one assumption which John Stuart Mill enunciated better than anyone else about a century ago. The definition has two interdependent parts. On the one hand, democracy means that the majority of citizens are the proper determiners of every policy and practice. On the other hand, democracy means that the minority of citizens have the unrestricted privilege of criticizing openly and seeking to persuade the majority at any time that one or another adopted policy requires modification and possibly repudiation.

What, more exactly, does this democratic conception of control say to educational leadership? I think it says several important things that too many of us are not yet fully prepared in our hearts to accept. On the negative side, this polaristic conception of majority rule-minority dissent says that the school leader must use unfailing caution lest he allow his own position of control to exceed its rightful boundaries—in short, lest he, too, be corrupted by the temptations of power to which the history of leadership abundantly attests.

Also on the negative side, this concept says that we need to distinguish very clearly between the administration of education and the leadership of education. Granted that the distinction is not always empirically evident, the principle that separates the two is perfectly evident. The administrator of any enterprise is precisely defined as one who administers—that is, as one who implements policy. Thus the administrator as such neither makes educational policy nor determines the practices that follow from these policies. The majority does this—the majority of the community, in the first instance; the majority of personnel in the educational enterprise, in the second instance. The administrator has no business whatsoever, for example, to decide upon a curriculum policy or to authorize a particular course of study under that policy. This is the prerogative of the professional staff directly engaged in the work of the curriculum—that is, the practicing teachers.

The prevailing confusion of terminology and function leads me to propose the abolition of Departments of School Administration. For actually they are, or if not they ought to be, Departments of Implementation, departments devoted chiefly to the considerable skills essential to the effective carrying out of democratically established policies and plans.

Finally, the positive responsibilities of educational leadership become clear only when its controlling functions are once more redefined in the light of this distinction. Of course, education needs leaders, many more strong and competent ones than are now available. Meanwhile, although both the role of the implementer and the role of the leader may sometimes be combined in the same individual, often they are not—at least not well. It is, therefore, worth proposing that Departments of School Implementation be established adjacent to but clearly distinguished from Departments of School Leadership.

What then, by contrast with administrative or implementing functions, are the leader's necessary functions? They are epitomized in the Gestalt of concepts and commensurate obligations that constitute our charter:

The educational leader is, first, a *creative* leader. He generates original, deviant plans and ideas. He shares them with his constituency whenever he can, and he opens the door wide for others to generate and to try equally original, deviant plans and ideas.

The educational leader is, second, an *audacious* leader. He points well ahead of where his school is at any given time. He kindles the flame of the genuine utopian. He encourages the curriculum-maker and the school-designer to become, like himself, future-centered educators.

He is, third, a *directive* leader. He views education and he helps his associates to view it as the greatest of all human institutions, through which man learns to shape and to direct post-organic evolution.

He is, fourth, a *convergent* leader. He uses every opportunity in the classroom, the shop, the sports field, and the neighborhood to encourage human beings in all their uniqueness to converge into more communal and cooperative ways of working, playing, and living. By the same token, he supports the struggles of people everywhere to construct a union of nations under international and enforceable law.

He is, fifth a *committed* leader. Not only does he reveal openly his own value orientation, his own moral choices, but he tries to imbue education as a whole with the moral and esthetic qualities of religiosity. At the same time he insists upon scrupulous critical-mindedness toward every one of these qualities.

He is, sixth, a *confronting* leader. He is familiar with the most important findings of the scientists about the subjective and objective obstacles to personal and cultural development. He urges teachers also to confront these obstacles in practice as well as theory, and to provide uninhibited opportunity for their students to learn everything they can of the work of explorers in all the sciences of man.

He is, seventh, an *involved* leader. He tries constantly to translate ideas into action, to support experimental testing of projects, to draw his school directly into the channels of planned social change, and to encourage teachers to become a free, powerful, organized force within the total power structure of this and other nations. He is a leader, in short, dedicated to the partnership of strategic means and world-encompassing ends.

Insofar as this partnership results, he is, eighth and finally, a *controlling* leader. He controls by the paradox of rejecting personal power in favor of power vested entirely in those who constitute the organism of the democratic school-community.

Index

The Society for Educational Reconstruction

The Society for Educational Reconstruction (SER) is a voluntary non-political organization for encouraging personal, group, and social transformation through innovative and change-oriented education. It was founded in 1969. Its membership consists of concerned citizens and educators in many parts of the United States and elsewhere in the world, all committed to the purposes of SER and wishing to participate in activities designed to advance those purposes. Four central concepts shape the goals of SER:

1. Cooperative Power. SER is a support network for educators and citizens who function as social change activists. It encourages them to collaborate in order to assure that knowledge is being applied for moral purposes. It also seeks to aid them in overcoming the evil effects of agism, racism, sexism, and other types of unfair discrminiation in schools and society. SER members are involved in shared planning in order to achieve a better future for all humanity.

2. Global Order. Learning processes that respect human dignity and diversity are advocated by SER. Its members seek ways to end exploitation, violence, and nuclear proliferation in order to eradicate the chief causes of war by establishing social justice and world law. SER defends the rights of all to dissent and be different. It helps its members to transcend the limitations of narrow ideological and national allegiances in order to form a more global outlook encompassing all of humankind.

3. Self-transformation. Members of SER design and offer instruction that enhances the creative potential of both learners and teachers. They stress developing the skills needed for effective intercultural communication, conflict resolution, and mutual understanding. They work to reconstruct existing institutions so that those institutions will become more convivial and inclusive. They advocate learning experiences that promote holistic social selfhood.

4. Social Democracy. It is the contention of SER that educational and social decisions should be democratically made. Its members labor to achieve equal access to educational and employment opportunities for all. They urge corporations and government agencies to increase their socially beneficial activities and cease their harmful operations. They strive for a fairer distribution of the world's resources and wealth, as well as for ecologically-sound policies.

Persons who embrace these concepts are encouraged to join SER. Please use the form on the facing page for that purpose.

SER Membership Form

Name ______________________________

Profession ______________________________

Address ______________________________

____
(include Zip-code)

Type of Membership (please check your choice):

- ❑ Regular ($25 per year)
- ❑ Family ($35 per year)
- ❑ Full-time Student ($15 per year)
- ❑ Institution ($50 per year)

Please make checks for the amount indicated above payable to "The Society for Educational Reconstruction" and mail with this form to:

The Society for Educational Reconstruction
c/o Gaddo Gap Press
3145 Geary Boulevard, PMB 275
San Francisco, California 94118, U.S.A.